# Speed Bumps on the Road to Enlightenment

*By Janice J. Beaty, PhD*
*Julie Adams*

First Edition

cdp
CRYSTAL | DREAMS
publishing

Oshawa, Ontario

# Speed Bumps On The Road To Enlightenment
by Janice J. Beaty and Julie Adams

| | |
|---|---|
| Managing Editor: | Kevin Aguanno |
| Acquisitions Editor: | Sarah Schwersenska |
| Copy Editor: | Susan Andres |
| Typesetting: | Peggy LeTrent |
| Cover Design: | Troy O'Brien |
| eBook Conversion: | Agustina Baid |

Published by: Crystal Dreams Publishing
(a division of Multi-Media Publications Inc.)
Box 58043, Rosslynn RPO, Oshawa, Ontario, Canada, L1J 8L6.

http://www.crystaldreamspublishing.com/

All rights reserved. No part of this book may be reproduced or transmitted in any form or by any means, electronic or mechanical, including photocopying, recording or by any information storage and retrieval system, without written permission from the publisher, except for the inclusion of brief quotations in a review.

Copyright © 2009 by Crystal Dreams Publishing

| | | |
|---|---|---|
| Paperback | ISBN-10: 1-59146-066-2 | ISBN-13: 9781591460664 |
| Adobe PDF ebook | ISBN-10: 1-59146-221-5 | ISBN-13: 9781591462217 |
| Microsoft LIT ebook | ISBN-10: 159146-222-3 | ISBN-13: 9781591462224 |
| Mobipocket PRC ebook | ISBN-10: 159146-223-1 | ISBN-13: 9781591462231 |
| Palm PDB ebook | ISBN-10: 159146-224-X | ISBN-13: 9781591462248 |

Published in Canada. Printed simultaneously in the United States of America and England.

CIP data available from the publisher.

# Dedication

In memory of
Robbin Freer Armstrong

# Table of Contents

Introduction ................................................. 7
Chapter 1
   The Land Before Time ............................... 9
Chapter 2
   Your Higher Selves ................................. 27
Chapter 3
   Driving Without Headlights ................... 45
Chapter 4
   Life Lessons .......................................... 63
Chapter 5
   Detours .................................................. 81
Chapter 6
   Cosmic Humor ..................................... 103
Chapter 7
   Becoming a Metaphysical Junkie ......... 121
Chapter 8
   Are We There Yet? ................................ 135

**Chapter 9**
   Fasten Your Seatbelt .............................. 151

**Chapter 10**
   Help! I Got What I wanted ................... 169

**Chapter 11**
   I'm Not There Yet ..................................... 191

About the Authors ...................................... 213

# Introduction

This extraordinary book is a wake-up call for everyone to become aware of what is happening behind the scenes of life. We are in a transitional period as Earth and its inhabitants prepare for a major shift in consciousness. The shift can be a smooth one if enough people wake up and take charge of their lives or a bumpy one if they do not.

The major voice you hear as you read these chapters comes from a spiritual group known as the White Sisterhood. In straightforward terms, they explain who you are, how you got here, and how to overcome the "speed bumps" in your life such as guilt, fear, anger, abuse, apathy, grief, and judgment by bringing in the Light of Love.

The authors add examples from their own lives that validate these important insights. They invite you to "Fasten your seatbelts, and prepare for the ride of your life as loving beings from beyond the veil guide you on the trip of a lifetime—your lifetime. Let's go!"

*Speed Bumps on the Road to Enlightenment*

In the swirling cosmos
Appeared a light;
The dawn of creation,
The Spark of Life.
And so it began...

CHAPTER 1

# The Land Before Time—Where You Came From

Life is the ultimate road trip. It can be long or short, twisted and bumpy, or relatively smooth and easygoing. You humans are as different as night and day, and your life paths are a reflection of your individuality. Even though you all have your own road map with different routes marked, you all have two things in common: a beginning and an ending. Luckily, for you, no matter how confusing your path is, it will always lead you Home.

Beginnings and endings are the easy part. The long haul down the middle of life is the most difficult. One of the main keys to navigating your way on the road of life is knowing where you began…where you started. Our intent in this first chapter is to present you with an overview of how and where it all began.

## Beginnings of Creation

In the beginning, there was Consciousness, and out of Consciousness, matter was born. The creation of matter produced energy and magnetism, which in turn enlivened Consciousness. Consciousness used the energy to continue expanding and creating. So began the "Spark of Creation."

The Spark was Light, and Light was Love, and Love became Spirit. Spirit was formed as a reflection of Creator. In its truest essence, Spirit means reflection. Everything that was created had a Spark of the Prime Creator, the Source, God, in it. There are many such names and titles. In this writing, we are comfortable with "Creator."

Universes were created, and as the universes expanded, so too did Spirit. You may wonder why we mention "universe" in the plural and not the singular. You have known that there are many galaxies in what you thought was "the universe." In reality, there are galaxies within galaxies and universes within universes. There are, in fact, many dimensions of each.

Spirit, being a true reflection of Creator, created also. Spirit formed realms and dimensions and populated the new universes. Above all else, Creator craved knowledge. Out of the desire for knowledge, diversity was born. Everything that was created had its story to tell, knowledge to share. From a speck of dust to a brilliant star, each piece of creation had a life cycle.

## Creation of the Planets

All types of planets were created. Some were created to evolve and die as gas and vapor. Some were solid rocks or covered with vegetation. Many went through their evolutionary process with no habitation. Still other planets were inhabited by many species and civilizations of beings that were alike or all different. They were big; they were small; they were dense; or they were etheric. Some of these beings were composed

*The Land Before Time—Where You Came From*

of biological and mineral properties. Yes, there is a spark of truth in your sci-fi stories of androids or robot-like beings. Re-member[1], everything has a Life Spark of Creator within it. Even rocks and minerals are live entities.

    These beings interacted and evolved with their planets. They were all different but connected with a common theme. Their existence was created for knowledge. As the universes expanded and evolved, the information superhighway came into being. The spiritual realms were created to house the great libraries and halls for the storage of knowledge. Spirit gathered the knowledge back to the Halls of Records where Spirit studied what did and did not work. If something did not work out as planned, it was not destroyed but allowed to live out its life cycle. And all continued to evolve to become the perfect reflection of Creator, which is Love, the Spark of Life.

## The Swirling Cosmos

Creation is timeless and endless: a spiral or a circle. Since Spirit is the perfect reflection of Creator, everything that Spirit creates becomes one with Creator again when its life cycle ends. And as Creator is always creating, a part of that energy goes back out into creation again.

    The common theme of all creation is knowledge, and the common thread is Love, that piece of Creator in all things that brings them back to the Source. The spark of creation always comes back into itself in an endless circle. Within that circle is the beginning and ending of any life or thought. It is the now.

---

[1] See p. 123 for an explanation of this spelling.

## Creation of Planet Earth

All of the galaxies and planets had a Spark of Creator in them, but the planet Earth was special and unique. Not only was Earth a grand experiment, it was a grand gift. Creator created Earth as a gift for himself. Earth was endowed with more than just a Spark of Creation. It was created to house the *feminine* aspect of Creator. All of the other planets were a combination of science, technology, and life. But Earth *was* life, a huge, wonderful, sentient being—Mother Earth. She lived, she breathed, and she healed. Earth was fertile, passionate, birth giving, and nurturing. She was/is the Heart of the Universe.

The Earth was a special planet and therefore needed special beings to inhabit her. So the human race was created as a reflection of her feminine energy. The first Earthlings were peaceful, gentle, and endowed with reproductive capabilities.

Many of the other planets had beings that were either engineered or etheric in form, or a combination of both. Many were endowed with the male-dominant, ego-based, aggressive aspect. Others were a blend of masculine and feminine. But the people of Earth were created to reflect and embody the passive, love-based energy of the feminine, which was well and good—a loving, giving society of people who were destined to live and thrive there. And they did. They were the Lemurians.

## The Lemurians

The Lemurians inhabited a rich and fruitful continent in the middle of the Pacific Ocean. Their civilization was based on love for all living things, even rocks. Some of their megalithic stonework still survives on Easter Island, Pohnpei (Nan Modol), underwater off the coast of Japan, and in the high Andes. Many of the plants and some of the animals they developed still exist on Earth today: breadfruit, bananas, the coconut palm, fruit doves, fruit bats, llamas, and the lemur.

The Lemurians evolved for thousands of years. But they were not the only ones evolving. Mother Earth was evolving, too, and their continent was breaking up in the first great shift. They tried to use their energy to hold it together, but the energy of Mother Earth was more powerful. Still the Lemurians did not try to leave because they thought they could save their continent with their collective energies. They could not. Consequently, the majority of them perished, leaving only remnants of their civilization scattered along the coasts of what are now South and Central America and Southeast Asia and on the mountaintops of certain Pacific islands. As their civilization perished, so did much of the feminine energy that was balancing the Earth.

## The First Planet of Free Will

However, not only was Earth created to house the Mother energy, it was also designated as the first planet of free will. There were no strictures set. No rules were imposed. So Earth became the focal point of the universe. All eyes were on her.

Not all civilizations watching Earth were kind and benevolent. There were many of a negative nature, since Creator needed to see and experience all aspects including the negative. There were planets that were very hostile and warlike, governed with strict control. That was their purpose, to be the balance: good/bad, light/dark. But Spirit underestimated their aggressiveness, and it was becoming difficult to maintain the balance.

So there was Earth. Earth was the "Motel 6" of the cosmos with a giant neon sign reading, "Come Stay with Me." The original purpose of the Earth people was to interact and evolve with their star cousins, which they had done successfully until the demise of Lemuria. Now re-member, because Earth was a planet of free will, anyone could come there, even the black sheep of the family. And they did.

## Speed Bumps on the Road to Enlightenment

Most of these dark star cousins blended with the people on Atlantis, a subculture of Lemuria that lived on a huge continent in the Atlantic Ocean. This blended group thrived for thousands of years, but eventually, after Lemuria perished, the negative traits of the dark star cousins became dominant. The Atlantian people began embracing technology without Love. This was the first fatal error in the evolution of Earth.

These dark star cousins took advantage of the imbalance after the Earth's first great shift broke up the Lemurian continent. The very nature of the few survivors was passive, which made them susceptible to control by their aggressive, chaos-oriented cousins. Consequently, the dark cousins rearranged their biology. In effect, they cut the people's umbilical cord to the Earth Mother. The dark cousins tampered with human DNA, allowing them to control and enslave. Humans became their pawns. They had their own agendas, and the evolution of Earth and the spreading of the Love vibration was not one of them.

Are we saying, then, that beautiful Earth was set up to entice negative star beings to your peaceful planet? Yes. Creator was unable and unwilling to destroy any of his creations, no matter how unruly they behaved. Instead, he dangled the succulent plum of Earth in front of them in order to draw them in so that their violent masculine energy could be transmuted by the feminine energy of their Earth cousins. As you know, it did not work out as planned. Instead, this dark energy eventually caused the destruction of Atlantis and the second great Earth shift.

Originally, Earth was a planet completely devoid of aggressive energy. In theory, such a high concentration of the feminine Love energy seemed like the perfect solution to balance the aggressive energy of the universe. But the power of the dark cousins was underestimated. The subjugation of the human race was not a malicious intent but rather a consequence brought on by the lack of knowledge.

## Preserving Lost Knowledge

It was a dark time after the fall of Atlantis. Even though the impact of the aggressive energy upon humans was miscalculated, your true purpose was not lost. Spirit had placed other beings on Earth to preserve your lost knowledge for you. They were the whales and dolphins. These highly evolved, Mother-encoded beings resonating with the Love vibration have been the keepers of your heritage for millennia. Hidden away under the waters of Earth, they are treasure chests of knowledge waiting to come open when the time is right.

Let's not forget the benevolent star cousins who had been watching your trials and wanted to help but could not interfere on your planet of free will. Instead, they sent you cosmic lightning bursts of Love and enlightenment. This short-circuited the negative genetic engineering in a few strong souls, allowing them to maintain their connection with Mother Earth.

Some of these benevolent star cousins also volunteered to be born into the Earth's culture and to carry within them the seeds of the lost knowledge. Those seeds were brought repeatedly, and it has been your choice to see, to feel, and to make use of them. Earth is your birthright. She is your Mother and your mentor. This is your history, your beginning.

## Universal Melting Pot

Earth is also the melting pot of the universe, and one country was destined to be its prime example. It is no coincidence that the United States has become such a powerful nation in so short a time. It is a reflection or mirror of what this planet was intended to be—a place where all the star cultures could

*Speed Bumps on the Road to Enlightenment*

come and evolve and carry the feminine aspect of Creator back to their home planets. In no other spot on this Earth is the blending of cultures more predominant than in the United States.

Carrying the Love vibration out to the universe is the primary goal of all the people of Earth. The people of the United States are supposed to be the shining examples of the blending of cultures, a living testament of the feminine, Love-based energy.

The people on Earth are not only representatives of the Earth nations but they are also representatives of the galactic nations. You are like trees that have been grafted to bear different varieties of fruit. You are human, spirit, and extraterrestrial beings all in one. You carry the seeds of many nations within you. Your common goal is to harmonize the masculine energy with the feminine Love vibration to bring about balance. Even though the process has taken longer than planned, it will happen in time. It is happening now.

## The Role of Animals

A horse is a horse, of course, of course…or is it? Many of you have never considered the spiritual impact on Earth of the animal kingdom. We previously mentioned whales and dolphins, but all of the animals have a special role. They are, in fact, very special spiritual beings in their own right and move through evolution just as you do. They were put here to help maintain balance on Earth.

Re-member, Earth is a living thing that feeds on more than energy, rain, and sunlight. The decomposition of vegetation and biological matter feed the Earth by replacing nutrients and minerals. Certain creatures and organisms within nature also feed upon the wastes and toxins produced by mankind. Although there is already knowledge of these helpful organisms, much of it has been suppressed by commercial interests. As you transmute the last remnants of the dark cousin's influence, this suppressed knowledge will also become known.

The animal kingdom grows and learns through the same evolutionary process as you do. The more highly evolved the animal spirit is, the more it interacts with its fellow inhabitants. Yes, that means you. Some of these wonderful animal beings actually contract to come in with you. It is no coincidence of nature when a special pet enters your life. It comes as a loving reminder of where you came from.

## The Pet Connection

The loving companionship of a pet is often what helps you get over a difficult speed bump on your life path. Children especially need these loving beings. When you are living your contract as children, you feel and express with Love and trust. But Love and trust are not necessarily what you get in return. It is during these trials that loving animals often appear and interact with you.

Animals also allow angels to occupy their bodies briefly. There have been many times throughout your history when animals have suddenly appeared in times of great need. Often animals will contract to reincarnate with you through several lifetimes.

Dogs are some of these evolved beings. They are here to give you a living testament of unconditional Love. Even when dogs have been abused and neglected, they will still look at you with Love. They see you as who you really are—beautiful, loving, spiritual beings. Dogs are visible examples of the lesson of forgiveness, which you all must learn. Julie, one of the authors of this book, has a story to tell about a dog of hers.

> **Julie's Saint Bernard**
>
> As a child growing up, my family and I had a Saint Bernard called Sappho. The dog expressed her Love for my brothers and me by being very protective of us. We used to wade and swim in the Susquehanna River. When we went out where the water came over our knees, she would grab us by the seat of our swim pants and pull us back to shore. In the winter, when we went sled riding, she would grab us by our boots and stop us from going too fast.
>
> The Love bonds were so strong between us that even after she died, we all saw her spirit in our backyard. We would hear her scratch at the back door to be let in. When we opened the door, we could hear her footsteps scuff across the floor. Then we would hear her lean against the wall and slide down into her favorite spot and give a big sigh of contentment. She continued doing this almost daily for two months after she had physically left Earth. I'll never forget Sappho.

## Cats That Saved Me

Cats are another facilitator. They feed on negative energies and transmute them to positive energies. When negative situations are occurring, there are discordant vibrations in the air around them. Cats sense this and can change the vibrations with their fur. Have you ever noticed how a cat's fur moves and twitches? Each hair is a minute sensor that picks up the negative vibrations. The twitching movement essentially breaks up the vibration and dispels it. Julie also has remarkable stories to tell about two cats in her life.

# The Land Before Time—Where You Came From

> In my early teens, when I was consumed with deep depression from the physical, emotional, and sexual abuse I was suffering, I would escape by taking long walks up the mountain behind our house to a special place in the woods. As I walked, my cat Parrot would climb up on my shoulder, pat me on the cheek, purr in my ear, and lick the tears from my face. Parrot and I would sit within the arms of forest until I felt peace.

When I was in my mid-thirties, divorced and living on my own, a beautiful golden-haired cat I called Fanny presented herself to me. It was love at first sight. Fanny had some health problems that I was very diligent about taking care of for her. After I had Fanny for about five years, I had to have a physical exam myself for a job. It was discovered that I had a heart murmur. I made an appointment to see a specialist in two weeks. One morning, a week before my appointment, I woke up and noticed Fanny lying on the floor with glazed eyes and breathing difficulty. I immediately rushed her to the vet, where she was diagnosed with a class-four heart murmur, which had not been there previously. She had to be put to sleep. The next week at my doctor's appointment, he found that my own heart murmur had completely disappeared. He couldn't believe it. It was then I realized that Fanny's Love for me was so strong she had taken my heart murmur onto herself.

## Unicorns and the Fairy Realm

The unicorns of your folklore are not creatures of fiction. These beautiful, magical beings are the angels of the animal kingdom. The unicorns were actually on the physical Earth plane in the beginning but moved into another dimension when the dark cousins came to Earth. These invaders did not realize the deep connections between humans and animals for they were unfamiliar with the bonds of Love energy.

Unfortunately, the invaders did appalling genetic experiments blending animals and humans, as has been described by your seer Edgar Cayce. These blendings are recorded in your mythology. But the bulk of the animal kingdom was spared this genetic manipulation because the unicorns placed a shield of protection around them. The fact that the star cousins could not affect all the animals helped to maintain the balance and the Love connection on Earth.

Unicorns function on pure Love. That is why they are described in your folklore as interacting with abused and lonely children. Medieval art also shows unicorns in conjunction with maidens who represented purity.

Unicorns are part of a greater community on Earth—the fairy realm. Unlike humans, the fairy realms can move between dimensions. The unicorns hold the magic for these realms. The fairies, of which there are many species, are the caretakers of nature. They are bright, light, and full of mischief. They have limited interaction with humans, much preferring to dance in a field of daisies. Their boundless joy and Love for Mother Earth is what keeps nature blooming in an often negatively repressive atmosphere. The fairies, elves, elementals, and nature sprites balance the negative energy produced by man against nature. All your cultures on Earth have stories in their folklore of these elusive beings.

## Indigenous People

Native Americans and other indigenous cultures from around the world have long been aware of the role played by nature. It is often the foundation of their belief systems. They know, for instance, that the balance, the harmonizing, of all things is reflected in nature. They have studied the different aspects and

## The Land Before Time—Where You Came From

personalities of animals and have incorporated them into their cultures.

The native peoples are the remnants of the first Earth people. These ancestors of yours were the ones who received the cosmic lightning, enabling them to carry within themselves the fragments of the original Earth code. To avoid manipulation by your dark star cousins, they scattered and remained virtually hidden. As the population of Earth eventually expanded, these hidden sects of people were discovered.

Your history tells the story. It is well documented how these cultures were nearly, or often completely, decimated. The negative star energy was very strong in the world and did not want the knowledge that these people possessed to be shared. But history is changing. The tide of negative, aggressive, fear-based energy is turning. The gentle, loving, feminine energy is emerging again.

Look at the awareness that has come about in recent years concerning the abuse of native peoples. Love and understanding are now projected toward them. Negative energy is still around, but it is more balanced with the positive than before. It has been a long struggle for mankind as a whole, but the individual processing of all your life lessons has enabled this to come about.

## Star Cousins and Storytellers

Many references to the star cultures came to your planet. They are in the earliest cave drawings, the ancient Sumerian texts, and even in your Bible. All of the ancient tablets and manuscripts mention races of giant insect-like and serpent-like beings. Many of these races were not mentioned in favorable terms. They were the dark star cousins. They established control over Earth people, both physically and mentally. They assumed god-like status. Along with remnants of written knowledge that

*Speed Bumps on the Road to Enlightenment*

exist about these early races, they are also depicted in ancient artwork from around the world.

Numerous wars were fought between these star people here on Earth. The victors of these wars each imposed their own set of rules and ideology upon the human race. You were thought of as a conquered people, and you would have been, if not for the seeds.

The storytellers carried the seeds of the ancient knowledge. For a long period, there were no written languages, at least none that could be re-membered. All knowledge was transmitted orally. The storytellers were highly prized members of their tribes, often receiving as much respect as the shamans—the healers and wise ones.

The storytellers and the shamans often lived and worked together. In some cases, they were the same person. The storytellers carried the memories, the lore of their people. They were the key to the forgotten knowledge. The shamans were the doors. They had the magic to draw in the knowledge to heal and guide their people. Janice, one of the authors of this book, was a storyteller in many lifetimes. She was a carrier of the memories. Julie, the other author, was a healer and wise woman. As they did before, they are once again presenting knowledge for the enlightenment of man.

Once the dark cousins had planted their own seeds of negativity, they had no more interest in Earth. It was the act of war and conquering that they thrived on. Once they believed you were a conquered race, they left.

But we must remind you again that not all of the star visitors were negative. Many who came here were more in tune with nature than with man. They were able to move dimensionally, the same as the fairy realm. These are the more physically dense beings from the fairy realm still found on Earth today: the Sasquatch or Bigfoot people, the leprechauns, and the trolls. They also have limited contact with humans, preferring the solitude of nature.

## Angels and the Soul Realm

Angels are the workforce of the cosmos. They receive the thoughts or Sparks from the Creator and build with them. Some angels oversee galaxies, stars, and planets. Others are guardian angels who send you loving messages of encouragement. There are numerous levels and dimensions to the angelic realms.

One of these realms is where souls begin and end their journey. This realm is like a huge school, starting at the nursery level and never ending. The nursery area is where you prepare to begin your life's journey. You learn about where you are going and meet whom you will be traveling with through life. When you come back from a life trip, there are centers for healing and reflection, which clear you for your next journey. We will delve into this subject in the next chapters.

Some of the schools of learning are for souls who incarnate from other planets. Re-member, Earth is the planet of free will, unique among them all. Millions of souls in this realm were originally from other galaxies and planets.

The healing centers and Halls of Knowledge are there for you always. As you evolve and become more enlightened, you travel to these places in your dreams or in altered states such as astro-travel, meditation, or hypnotic trance. There are many such avenues. The roads of your lives are many, but your final destination is the same for all—Home. It just takes time.

## Time, a Twisting Road

"Once upon a time..." Is that not how fairy tales go? Fairy tales are works of fiction, like time, and they do not exist...or so you believe. In reality, time is a living thing—the part of creation that seems to hold everything together...or to stretch it apart. In order for Creator to get the true knowledge of any one event, it must be reflected in all its possibilities. Even during the creation of your world, in the sprouting of the first trees, there were endless possibilities. What would have happened if that first tree had been a different one? Would it not have changed the first forest? In different dimensions, every tree gets the support to be that first tree to see how it will affect the outcome.

Any thought or situation can have a hundred, a thousand, a million different endings. This is true even in your own life—if you had changed just one word in one conversation, look at all the possible outcomes and the effect it could have had on everyone else. But it takes time.

Time is the road that runs through the dimensions. It twists and turns like the switchbacks on mountain roads. What was in front of you for one second is now over your shoulder. The intersections on this endless road are a combination of past, future, and possibilities, a new timeframe called "the now."

The chapters to follow may help you to navigate this bumpy road of life. At least, they will tell you what twists and turns you can expect. The rest is up to you.

*The Land Before Time—Where You Came From*

*Speed Bumps on the Road to Enlightenment*

Father, mother,
Brother, wife;
Friend or foe
In peace or strife;
And so it was agreed…

CHAPTER 2

# Your Higher Selves: Drill Sergeants of the Universe

We start this chapter on a blank page—a sheet of white void of expression...or is it? In essence, it is already filled with possibilities, as were you at the moment of creation. You were specks of light, all very similar in color, but vibrating at slightly different frequencies. You were a blank page full of possibilities, waiting for the ink blood of life in order to write the words. You were tiny sparks of Creator, born with the thirst for knowledge and creating. You were also created with the intent to bring about balance between the negative- and Love-based energies on Earth.

You did not just leap to Earth in some haphazard group of humanity. Before incarnating on Earth, you studied the knowledge in the Halls of Records to see how the evolving process worked on other planets. This gave you a basis for what was to come. But you could not get a true picture of life on Earth, as the circumstances there were to be far different from anything else ever done.

*Speed Bumps on the Road to Enlightenment*

## Your Support System

The work on Earth was to be very difficult, so you set up a support system for yourselves. As individuals, you knew the work to be done on Earth would be impossible alone. So large groups of you combined your energies and became what we call "oversouls." Before combining, each Spirit broke off a fragment of itself to become the incarnating soul. These fragments then combined into family groups to provide another means of support. The oversoul and the fragment, a full soul in its own right, remained connected at all times. Like a giant spider web, glowing threads of loving light connected you to your soul family and oversoul.

The family groups were composed of hundreds of individual souls. Some souls were in more than one family group, not unlike in-laws in marriage. With the different families having connections to different oversouls, you became part of a vast collective, a huge support group channeling you Love, light, and encouragement at all times.

In the beginning, large family groups came in as whole nations. As you have observed, there are many nations or cultures on Earth. For many lifetimes in the early years of your evolution, you reincarnated only within your own cultural group. This provided you with a stronger support system during the infiltration of the star cousins.

## Souls from Other Planets

Not all cultures there on Earth started at the same time. There is evidence of this found by your archaeologists. Even older civilizations than you thought possible will be discovered soon in the Polar Regions.

Many of the people on Earth were incarnate souls from other planets. Some nations comprised beings who came here in their spacecrafts. Similar in biology, they could blend right in, and that is what you did. You all blended—physically, mentally, spiritually—into one soul with a thousand different faces.

## Your Contract

The first thing to appear on your blank sheet was a contract. The individual souls of the family group agreed to help one another through their life lessons. Like a huge Shakespearian play, everyone chose their parts: parents, siblings, friends, lovers, and enemies. Anyone who could even remotely affect your life lessons chose a part. This is the hardest thing for you to understand today—that you chose the circumstances of your life, the bad along with the good.

Re-member, the purpose of creation is to gain knowledge. To gain knowledge, you need to experience all: love, hate, fear, pain, joy, poverty, riches, etc. You may study each of these aspects of being, but you cannot truly feel the essence of the emotion created unless you live it. It is living these life lessons that enable you to evolve into the true reflection of Creator.

## Your Oversouls

As you evolved on Earth and moved through your lessons, so too did your oversouls. They shifted and reorganized to assist you in the work you were doing. Initially, it was just survival. But later, you became healers, writers, and artists. Your oversouls became patrons of the arts. Each group became a sponsor of a specific field of endeavor. Healers came from the healing oversoul. Musicians came from the musician oversoul.

It is out of these concentrated spheres of knowledge that prodigies were born. The great thinkers and artists of your world were and are members of these oversouls—highly evolved beings such as Plato, Pythagoras, Mozart, and, most dear to Janice, Mark Twain. Twain came from the oversoul of writers. His unique style of writing promoted the importance of the joy you need to glean from the simple things in life. When he left this Earth, part of his oversoul joined him and became the Mark Twain oversoul, so that other writers could benefit from the concentrated knowledge he had to share. Many such prodigies became oversouls to hold the knowledge for you to use.

## Your Higher Self

The human soul is but a microscopic part of the whole. The larger aspect of your soul is called your higher self—the part of you that is in the oversoul, the infinite you. If you re-member from Chapter 1, we told you about the dimensions of existence and the circle of time. In reality, you on Earth are experiencing the past, present, and future simultaneously. We know this concept of living time is difficult for you to comprehend. But on the three-dimensional Earth plane, time is linear and appears to move in only one direction, when in reality, it flows in all directions and through all the dimensions.

Even if you only choose one life lesson, it is played out with different aspects of yourselves in all the dimensions. These aspects of you are connected to your higher selves. Your higher selves are more difficult taskmasters than anyone you will ever meet in your lifetime. The lesson or lessons you set up for yourselves are daunting. You are the true examples of the expression "brave souls."

## The Birth Process

There is much Love, support, and encouragement for you in the angelic realm. You are highly honored for the difficult work you do in becoming human. Just being encased in a human body is scary enough to send some souls back Home. When you first incarnate, you slip into and out of the unborn child who is you until you grow accustomed to the new surroundings. Even as a fragment of your higher self, your light is enough to fill a whole room.

When you enter biology, you must pull your energy in and concentrate it. Once you become familiar with the birth process, after several incarnations, you may decide to wait next time and enter at the moment of birth. This is only one tiny decision you have to make before being born.

## Suicide

There are lifetimes when you become a little overzealous and choose something too difficult to accomplish, or you are so eager to begin a lesson that you come into life at the wrong moment. This often leads to suicide by your own hand or by placing yourself in a situation where someone else will take your life. These souls are honored for what they attempted to do and are counseled before coming into life again.

There has been much stigma attached to suicide by your religious leaders. HEAR US NOW: THESE SOULS ARE HONORED AND LOVED! They are not loved less than souls that have completed their lesson. Not all suicides are spontaneous. Often a suicide is part of a life choice made by that soul and its soul family. Re-member, all things must be experienced.

*Speed Bumps on the Road to Enlightenment*

## Reincarnation and Karma

The process of multiple lives is called reincarnation. It is coupled with another term, karma, which is more easily explained by example. If in one lifetime you had been a slave owner, you might be the slave (or at least in some situation where you do not control your own life) when you reincarnate in the next life. Karma is like the saying "an eye for an eye" from the Old Testament of your Bible, only it is played out over several lifetimes.

You have felt that you would never get out of this karmic cycle—that you would always be making up for your past transgressions. But this is not so. Many of you have ended your karmic ties in recent years. Look at the number of divorces, or friends and families who have moved on to different lives. There have been many endings to lifelong associations because karma is no longer necessary. Re-member, you are part of a soul family, a collection of intelligences.

For millennia, life lessons have been brought back into the family groups. Each group consists of hundreds and thousands of souls. Multiply this by the number of years of a soul's existence, and you have an astronomical amount of knowledge that has been gathered. When a group contains all the knowledge of the life situations, karma is over. You are nearly all at this point today, and life will soon reflect the release of this negative shadow. When there is no karma, there can only be Love among you. Author Julie has a story about one of her early lives.

## Life on Another Planet

"My second husband John and I share a past life memory of when we were together on another planet. We re-member lying in a beautifully ornate tent upon blue sand dunes…yes, I said blue…at the edge of a sea. There was a longhaired, camel-type animal tethered nearby. We were gazing out the open tent flap at two blue moons, side by side in the twilight sky. We both received this image at the same time in this life while we were sitting together and talking, and we were surprised to be able to finish the other's sentences when describing it to each other. It is a memory I will cherish forever."

## Higher Selves as Drill Sergeants

In the title of this chapter, we have likened your higher selves to drill sergeants. By this, we mean your higher selves keep you focused on the goal, the ultimate completion of the lesson. If your higher selves did not keep your focus on the results, many of you would never agree to incarnate again. Life can hold many trials and scare off even the bravest of souls. It is extremely difficult to leave a place of such peace and harmony as your celestial Home and go to a land full of such disharmony as Earth. Your higher selves are not ruthless. On the contrary, their Love is boundless. Your Love is boundless. You are one and the same.

## Windows of Opportunity to Leave

When setting your contracts, you always make sure to write in "windows of opportunity" to leave the Earth plane. These windows appear during extremely difficult lessons in case you feel you cannot complete the contract. They also come at the end of lessons in case you are too fatigued to go on with further lessons. They are spaced out over your lifetime, and there is no shame attached if you choose to leave through any one of them.

You are in constant contact with your higher selves. It is in the dreamtime that you commune, although you seldom re-member this when you awaken. You view your progress and see what obstacles have entered your path. Re-member, this is a planet of free will, and many paths cross your own. Situations may occur that overshadow your original contract. A lesson of greater value may present itself, or you may simply decide that the time is not right after all. Contracts are rewritten many times. The common theme may be carried through, but it may be in much gentler terms.

## Near-Death Experiences

Author Julie wrote in such a window to open when she was only three years old. At that time, she had a near-death experience. The window was set up then so she could decide if she wanted to continue this particular life that would be filled with much abuse. She decided to stay. During the near-death experience, Julie and her higher self set up a safe place where her soul could go during the times of abuse. Even though the physical body still endured the abuse, her inner soul did not have to feel the invasion. Although she was aware of the abuse, the impact was filtered through the nervous system, and it came to her as second-hand knowledge. The softening of this information allowed her to deal with it more objectively and be able to work through the lesson.

Any window of opportunity can become a near-death experience. Some are for protection, as in Julie's case. Others are trigger points and opportunities to gain some healing and encouragement from Home. The human body can become so damaged and clogged that the soul inside cannot receive the loving vibrations from Home. A near-death experience can provide the body and the soul a time for healing.

Many people who have had near-death experiences have led brutal lives. After the experience, they often become advocates against the type of life they were leading. The reverse is also true. Some people have flowed through life seemingly carefree. When these people have near-death experiences, they usually step into a contract of human service with strong convictions. Your higher self orchestrates these contracts with

## *Your Higher Selves: Drill Sergeants Of The Universe*

you on a never-ending basis. You are the choreographer of your destiny, and your contracts help keep you in step through the changing tunes.

# Walk-Ins

We have discussed group contracts and individual contracts, but there are also shared contracts. These shared contracts can be expressed in several different scenarios. The one thing they all have in common is that more than one soul is using a particular body. The first of these scenarios involves "walk-ins." A walk-in is a soul that is contracted to take over a body for another soul who wants to leave. Some contracts for walk-ins can be set up prior to birth, and others are set up during the soul's incarnation. The residing soul can come to a point that it feels it can no longer stay in that particular life, or it may leave to enter a new contract for a period of learning. No matter the reason for the contract, the life of the person must be preserved.

Walk-ins are like understudies for actors. The play would not be the same if one of the characters came up missing. The part must be filled so that all roles may come into play. You all come into life to learn lessons for the gathering of knowledge. In the setting of your contract, you also come into life to assist others with their lessons.

When setting contracts for a new lifetime, an aspect of you may still be incarnate in a previous life or going through the healing/learning process between lives. In this case, a member of your soul family will incarnate for you until you can come and play your part. When the time is right, you walk into your contract, becoming the same age as the person who was holding the body for you.

This transition often occurs during a traumatic event that causes the original person to retreat into herself or himself

## Speed Bumps on the Road to Enlightenment

or during an illness where the body goes through periods of unconsciousness. The transference of the souls usually takes a few days. As in near-death experiences, the person going through the change will afterward exhibit different qualities. With walk-ins, there is usually more than just changes in thoughts and personality. There are subtle and sometimes not-so-subtle physical changes.

The incoming soul brings its own set of impressions with it, which is sometimes expressed in physical characteristics such as speech patterns, mannerisms, coordination, and physiological changes. Yes, walk-ins can look different from the original soul. Their faces may appear different. Often, eye color will change. Sometimes the transition will occur over several years, so the changes are not as noticeable. During these lengthy transitions, the two souls will take turns occupying the body and may often coexist for periods.

This brings up another type of shared contract. The incarnate soul will step back and allow another soul to enter and occupy the body with them. On a conscious level, the incumbent soul is often not aware of the visitor. Janice has a personal and up-close example of this type of contract to share with you.

### Mark Twain Walks In

My second husband Dale came to look exactly like Mark Twain. In 1982, before I met him, something traumatic happened to him. He became divorced, lost his well-loved job of many years, and as a result lost his home and most contact with his grown children all at once. He went through a short period of deep depression, after which he seemed to be changed dramatically. He didn't know this himself until people in Missouri, where he lived, began saying he looked exactly like Mark Twain. By 1983, he was invited to play Mark Twain's role in the annual Tom Sawyer Days in Hannibal, Missouri. Soon he was appearing as Mark Twain on different riverboats on the Missouri and Mississippi Rivers.

He knew very little about Mark Twain but decided he'd better find out. So he took a course on Mark Twain in Hannibal and then began visiting Mark Twain sites around the country to talk with people about the great humorist. He had the strong feeling that he was supposed to help bring back Twain's humor to ordinary people everywhere, especially in nursing homes and schools. In addition, he also had the overwhelming desire to learn about Mark Twain's (Samuel Clemens') family, in particular, his wife Livy, from Elmira, New York.

So there I was one afternoon in May 1986, in my early childhood education office at Elmira College where I taught, when this strange man who was the spitting image of Mark Twain walked through the door. He had been sent from the main office to see me because I taught a summer course on "Storytelling Mark Twain Style," and the other Mark Twain scholars on campus were nowhere to be found that day. He said that he was in Elmira to learn more about Mark Twain's family and had heard that his wife Livy often edited his written work. Was that true?

Whoa! The first thing I felt upon seeing the man was a bolt of electricity that went through me from head to toe! Who was he? Yes, of course I knew about Livy's editing of Twain's books. I knew all about Mark Twain. I had not only read all of his many books and spent hours at Twain's summer home Quarry Farm on top of East Hill above Elmira, I was also the only faculty member who was a native of Elmira. Elmira was the place where Mark Twain had married and was buried, the place where his children had been born, and where he had spent over twenty summers writing his most famous books. But who was this man standing in front of me?

I ended up taking Dale around to the various Twain sites in Elmira, telling him more about Twain than he ever wanted to know; inviting him to my summer storytelling class; and, later, traveling with him during every college break for the next five years; writing and publishing three books with him; and eventually marrying him! Of course, I had fallen in love with him from the very first moment he walked through the door. From the start, I realized Dale was more than a Mark Twain look-alike.

**Who was Dale?**

Here he was, this serious "transportation man"— this transportation law practitioner who knew little about Twain and would say nothing about his own past. But when he got on a stage to deliver Mark Twain anecdotes, he became a different person. A sense of humor seemed to bubble up from hidden depths, and even his eyes changed. Photos I took of him as this Victorian-looking gentleman in a dark suit, and then the smiling Mark Twain in his white suit, even showed him as two different persons."

## Your Higher Selves: Drill Sergeants Of The Universe

That's what he was. Two different persons...and never the twain shall meet, I might add. He was very uncomfortable with this Mark Twain persona of his and didn't really want to talk about it. During our travels together, when we were close in the evening, talking about everything under the sun, he was Mark Twain. Next morning when we met for breakfast, he was Dale again and didn't even re-member what he had told me the night before!

Some people asked him if he believed in reincarnation, because the resemblance was so striking. He didn't. I did, but I kept my mouth shut about it. So who was he? Most people actually treated him as if he truly was Mark Twain. They gave him gifts from Twain's past, told him where to go to find little-known Twain sites, and were so delighted to meet him they just couldn't get over it. With children, it was love at first sight. They rushed over to hug him, and some women even ran their fingers through his hair!

I took it all in. What I decided was this—Dale Janssen was indeed a Mark Twain walk-in. I knew about walk-ins from reading Ruth Montgomery's metaphysical books. But the only problem was that Dale, the original soul, had never walked out! I never did talk to Dale about ideas such as reincarnation and walk-ins because he was too straight-laced and conservative.

Dale and I were finally married in July 1990. Six months later, in January 1991, Dale collapsed on the sidewalk and left Earth for good. Where is his body buried? In the same Elmira cemetery as Mark Twain's! When did I find out the real truth of the matter? Just now, from this channel...a few paragraphs ago!

> If ever I doubted there was more to life than we are led to believe, my five extraordinary years with Dale Janssen convinced this serious college professor otherwise. Dale was a phenomenon! My involvement with the metaphysical side of life began with the jolt of Dale's death and has continued unabated ever since.

## Delayed Contracts

We thank Janice for this input, as we know that memories of Dale are very emotional for her. Lastly, we will discuss delayed contracts.

Sometimes a contract cannot be completed in one lifetime because dramatic events have occurred to interrupt it. You write your future as you go, and things can change rapidly on the planet of free will. Wars, Earth changes, and all manner of cataclysmic events can claim lives in a short period. These sudden losses of life can affect whole karmic patterns. When key players in a life lesson are taken out of the act, often the remaining actors will continue life working through bit parts. When all the souls involved are again ready to incarnate together, similar contracts are rewritten to take up where the old ones left off. Julie has a story to tell about a delayed contract in her own life.

# Your Higher Selves: Drill Sergeants Of The Universe

**A Life During Biblical Times**

The last lifetime my husband John and I shared prior to this one was sometime in early Biblical times on Earth. Our names were Gideon and Sephra. Gideon was a gray-haired older man and Sephra was a young woman, probably in her twenties, but they had a very strong love for each other. They were nomadic people. Sephra was captured by a warring tribe and taken as a concubine by the leader. In the memory of this life, I can still see Gideon standing with tears of anguish running down his face, calling the name of his beloved Sephra. Though he searched everywhere, he never found her before he died. Sephra lived many years as a slave and concubine but never forgot her first love.

Hundreds of years passed before Gideon and Sephra were able to come together to finish out their contract. In this lifetime, Gideon took on the female aspects and became me, Julie, in order for Gideon to experience the sexual abuse that Sephra had suffered. Sephra took on the male aspects and became John, who experienced grieving the loss of a loved one in the death of his first wife. We chose this lifetime to come together again, but not to relive the anguishing moments of grief and separation between us that had happened in the past. Instead, we chose to experience these highly emotional situations separately.

Only when John had overcome the loss of his first wife, and I had dealt with my issues of abuse, were we able to join together as man and wife in this life. We are still living and writing the rest of our story.

*Speed Bumps on the Road to Enlightenment*

## Take Heart

Karma has caused most of the speed bumps on your road of life. Your contracts with your loving soul family members are the vehicles that have enabled you to overcome them. Take heart, the road is getting smoother. Your drill sergeant loves you!

*Your Higher Selves: Drill Sergeants Of The Universe*

*Speed Bumps on the Road to Enlightenment*

Where did I come from?

Why am I here?

Is there someone to guide me?

Anyone near?

And so it was forgotten…

CHAPTER 3

# Driving Without Headlights

Spirit has ensured that the knowledge of your past lives is available to you. It is recorded in the Akashic Records, which are stored in the Halls of Knowledge. All your earthly lives, the lives you lived on other planets, and the time you spent between lives is recorded there. Vast tomes of knowledge about every aspect of yourself and everything in creation are available to you. Spirit has also created beautiful places for healing. In these places, colors and sounds can be more than seen and heard. They can be felt and tasted. They are alive—as is everything.

    Spirit also sends you continuous vibrations of Love that embrace you throughout your whole life. These things are a part of you. The memories of Home are encoded in your very soul. You ask, "Why can't we re-member this?" There are two reasons, one of which we discussed in a previous chapter—the genetic engineering that the dark cousins imposed on you. The dark cousins disconnected ten of the twelve strands of your DNA. Your DNA is much more than a blueprint of your biology. It is the blueprint of the infinite you—the battery cables that connect you to All That Is and All That Will Ever Be.

## The Veil of Forgetfulness

The second reason is the veil of forgetfulness. Spirit placed the veil on you. Now consider what a veil is in your world. It is a light gauze fabric placed over the eyes that filters, softens, and adds a bit of mystery. This filtration, this mystery, was the intention behind the veil. If you had access to and knew about everything, what then would be the purpose of life? All souls who go into life have a veil about them. It is placed so you have to work for and experience the lesson. The veil is thin enough that, with a little effort, you can get inspirations as to how to work through a situation. The greatest gift we can ask for is for you to re-member…to join once again the disconnected parts of your memories.

One of the greatest distortions on this Earth plane is forgetting. Great beings have come onto the Earth plane to help you, and all they re-membered when they got here were small glimpses of why they came. Now it is up to you to re-member. Hearts are the main access to re-membering, not the brain. The brain cannot re-member everything. It does not hold the capacity to re-member without the heart.

## Realign Your Heart

So we say, bring back the heart. Bring up the heart. Realign your heart with your brain. Be aware that the heart is not in its right alignment. Realign. Realignment is a natural sequence that happens from desiring to re-member. Many of you have been invested in not re-membering due to the pain of lost hope. Many people are living substitute lives. Much of the Earth is living in substitute forms of the Creator. Now is the time to re-member and to realign.

*Driving Without Headlights*

Free will allows you the opportunity to use as much of or as little of this information as you want. Being human offers many new experiences, new ideals, and new healings. The plethora of human emotions alone is outstanding. Many souls who came into Earth had never been physical beings. Being able to feel anything was a seduction for many. Even though they knew how to access universal knowledge, free will allowed them not to.

You were so caught up in the passion, in the pleasure of living, that you lost sight of your intent, which was to harmonize the negative dark star energy with your own. When the dark cousins arrived, you were blindsided. When they disconnected your DNA, that intensified the veil. It left you driving down the highway of life with no headlights. Only brief and distorted images could get through, like the flickering moonbeams of a clouded sky.

## Guardian Angels and Spirit Guides

You have often felt that you are driving the darkened highway by yourself. You need to re-member that you are not alone. Your higher selves and the members of your soul family are with you always. Some members of your soul family come in as your spirit guides. They are not to be confused with your guardian angels. Angels almost never incarnate. They may take on the guise of a human at times to intercede on your behalf when another's life path comes perilously close to interrupting yours. Your angels' main purpose is to be your cheering squad. They surround you with the Love vibrations of Home and continuously shout words of praise and encouragement.

Your spirit guides, on the other hand, have often walked in your shoes and know the difficult road before you. They would not abandon you to drive the darkened highway alone. They hold your map for you. Since they are not in physical form, they do not have the veil of forgetfulness over them. They can see your path at all times, and like a seeing-eye dog, they give you nudges to keep you on the road.

## Recognize the Nudges

Learning to recognize these nudges is another means for the thinning of the veil. These nudges can manifest as a whisper on the wind, a prickle of gooseflesh, or as a bird flying across your path. They are engineered to draw your attention to the path you are on or to offer validation that the path you are on is correct.

When you start down a road that is different from the ones on your map, your guides place many obstacles in your path to try to divert you. If you fail to acknowledge these obstacles and bullheadedly plow your way through, you often find yourself on a very bumpy road. But when you heed these warnings, the road before you smoothes, and things fall into place more easily.

As we have told you before, you exist in the now. You are living your past, present, and future simultaneously. The veil of forgetfulness slips now and then, and you have what you call moments of déjà vu. They appear suddenly as the remembrance of a place, the recognition of an unfamiliar face, or familiar conversation. This déjà vu often leaves you with a tickle up your spine and a look of wonderment on your face.

## Coincidences: What Are They?

The greatest of these nudges are coincidences. They validate that the thoughts, words, or deeds that are occurring are in keeping with your life map. They show you the synchronicity of your actions. Janice has several stories to tell us about rather astounding coincidences in her own life.

*Driving Without Headlights*

"A coincidence is a miracle of God in which He wishes to remain anonymous" is a saying I have lived by most of my life. Everywhere I go and everywhere I have lived, the major events of my life have been announced by a coincidence. Most coincidences for me involve people. For instance, I met my first husband, Jim, in a very coincidental manner. He happened to get on a bus I was on in Kyoto, Japan, bound for the old imperial city of Nara. We were the only Americans aboard, and I knew him!

He was one of 300 American teachers back on the island of Guam, just as I was. But until that moment, in that strange setting, neither of us had paid any attention to the other. It was as if some unseen hand had reached out and dropped us into that bus…just at that moment…just in the far-off place…in a city of over a million people. Impossible! We ended up going out for dinner that evening, and we were married four months later.

**The Dale Coincidences**

Ten years later, after Jim passed away, I returned to the states and took up college teaching in Elmira, New York, my old hometown and an important Mark Twain site, as previously mentioned. In 1986, I happened to read a novel about Mark Twain coming back to Earth in 1985 to complete some of his unfinished business, 75 years after he had passed away, when Halley's comet appeared. Now the comet was visiting Earth again. The last chapter of the novel has him revisiting Elmira, taking a room at the Holiday

49

Inn along the river, walking over to Elmira College, and buying a notebook in the college bookstore.

As you re-member, the spitting image of Mark Twain, Dale Janssen, walked into my office in May 1986 after taking a room at the Holiday Inn, walking over to the college, and buying a notebook in the college bookstore. Thus began our own five years of coincidental adventures. Dale would go into a restaurant in St. Louis, for instance, and find out that a man at the next table was married to a woman whose great-grandfather had signed Mark Twain's pilot's license for navigating the Mississippi River. Of course, the man sent Dale a copy. Or Dale would apply for a post office box and be given one with the number 1601, a number unknown to either Dale or the postal clerk but very significant in Mark Twain's life, as it was the title of a sketch he had written. Or Dale and I would walk into a restaurant in Elmira and a man would say, "I have the doorknob to your father-in-law's [Livy's father's] house from when they dismantled it."

Often, five or six coincidences would happen to us in a day. We walked onto a brand-new riverboat in St. Joseph, Missouri, where Dale discovered that he knew the pilot from two years previously and also the honky-tonk piano player from before that, and I found out that the piano player had a daughter who worked in the dining services at Elmira College.

Then I re-membered I had actually been on this very boat five years earlier for a dinner cruise at a conference in Miami Beach! Two years later, when Dale and I visited Fort Myers, Florida, for my son Dave's wedding, we happened to stop at the boat basin just as this same riverboat was pulling up, piloted by a different pilot but one who also knew Dale! Tell me about coincidences!

## What Is a Coincidence?

"What is a coincidence, anyway? You could say it is a seemingly accidental bringing together of people or elements into an incredible synchronicity. But coincidences are not accidental. They are, in fact, special set-ups created for the people involved to stop and take notice. They say to us, 'Pay attention, something impossible has just happened or is about to happen. There is great meaning in this for you. Make the most of it.'"

"If coincidences truly are set-ups, then who has set them up, I wondered? Don't be too surprised at the answer: we have. We, ourselves, have set them up. Somehow, we people on Earth have become so blocked from our inner selves that our subconscious, with spiritual assistance, sets up these scenarios to wake us up to what is really going on around us. They seem to say to us, 'You are on the right track. You are going in the right direction.' Keep it up, the channeling group says."

## Coincidences Are Multidimensional

Coincidences are not of the mind, so do not look for them. It is their nature to be surprising. They go beyond the fringes of the mind and open you to being more than a single dimension—more than who you think you are in a single body. They are truly multidimensional…and so are you!

Coincidences are like little bridges, tunnels of light, or doorways, opening up people to their own spiritual realms. They are a part of a bigger network of energy than you realize. It is really about you people on Earth being larger than you think you are and validating this fact. A coincidence is the act of the Spirit inside of you and outside of you connecting. You need to become aware of it and observe your disbelief. "This can't be happening! How could this happen? It must be a coincidence. It can't be real!" But it is real. Coincidences are real.

## Coincidences Are Your Soul Speaking

A coincidence can allow energy to move that would otherwise remain still or stagnant. It is a release from the mundane. And whether you know it or not, part of you wants you to know you exist outside of the mundane. It is your opportunity to let the "ah-has" come in. Amuse yourself at your cynical disbelief as you observe these incredible happenings. Do not take them for granted. It is your soul sparking you…your soul that wants to push you through life…to help Love move into your life. It is like an energy that is generated from the soul to expand you and move the limits and limitations that are part of your life.

Coincidences invite you to come in…to open the door to magic…like the magical world of a child's eyes. You allow children to look for magic and fun. You observe children being entertained by seemingly miraculous happenings, but most of you do not allow magic and playfulness or even Love into your own lives. Love is magical and full of delight. It is part of the realm of wonder and wonderment. Coincidences are doorways to the knowing of the Spirit. And you have the power to open these doorways.

## Coincidences Are a Game for Adults

Some coincidences are signals to keep you alert for the next one. Some are directions for you to follow. Some are created to open up your thought areas or to give you information in a non-ordinary way. They are like a game for adults, a childlike game that breaks through your linear mind entrapment. Pay attention. Recognize that this is not what normally happens. Expand your consciousness of coincidences. Do not allow yourself to dismiss them. Give yourself permission to be open to them.

Many people on Earth are more open when they travel or go to a new place because they are not sure what it

*Driving Without Headlights*

will be like or what will happen. This is the time to be open for coincidences. You may want to state aloud your intent to receive coincidences, "I joyfully encourage happenings to occur even beyond my beliefs and expectations."

---

**Coincidences, Coincidences, Everywhere**

Janice continues...

Just before I sat down to write this chapter, a coincidence occurred that I didn't know about until now. I was having breakfast and reading from the *Smithsonian magazine*. I happened to open to the book reviews at the end, when my eye caught the title of a book—*I Thought My Father Was God, and Other True Tales of the NPR's National Story Project*. The project had collected over 4,000 submitted stories, of which, 179 appeared in that book. One-third was about families, a great many of which were about coincidences! What? I could hardly believe what I was reading!

The reviewer recounted one incident of a couple who first met when they were forced to sit together in a crowded restaurant. The girl finally gave the man her phone number, but he proceeded to lose it. Later that year, each of them, unknown to one another, traveled to Europe and, once again, found themselves sitting at the same table! This time, they finally fell in love and married. Whoa!

---

## The Coincidence Box

"But wait…there's more. The group we are channeling tells us more about coincidences. Julie is being shown a box with four sides, representing the four different sides of coincidences. They tell her that the first side is a person's initial reaction when a coincidence happens. Some people completely disregard it. Some people say, 'That's interesting,' but they don't take it any further."

### *The Second Side*

"The second side of the coincidence box makes some people look deeper. When they look deeper, Spirit enters their mind. It's like a direct knock on the door of the mind from Spirit. An instantaneous expansion of the mind takes place, making room for something else to follow. It might be an actual directional move or directional shift that will delay things or speed them up. For instance, something makes a person slow down and thus avoid an accident, keeps them from getting on a certain plane that later crashes, or keeps them sitting in a restaurant until someone significant shows up. It paves the way for something to happen later on because the set of circumstances is different after the shift."

### *The Third Side*

"The third side of the coincidence box relates to your destiny path…the road you must follow to enlightenment. It is one of the ways your guides and helpers get messages to you. A directional shift is sometimes connected to your destiny. After it occurs, it is good to say, 'What is this? Is there something else I need to see?' Open up, because you all need help with your contract that was agreed upon before you came to Earth. If you welcome divine help, you will receive more."

Too many people on Earth have been brainwashed into the concept of doing everything alone. You have cut yourselves off from your own spiritual help. It is part of the dark star cousins' plan of separation and opposition to unity. When there is unity, the dark cousins' followers do not have power. Their power lies in your separation from your soul group and your Creator. But you can change any time. A coincidence is a wake-up call to change.

### The Fourth Side

The fourth side of the coincidence box represents Love. Allow Love, whether it is coming from your own God-self or from others. Love produces coincidences. People seem to think Love does not include the intellect. They judge the word "Love" to be outside of their intellect.

Love is more than you think it is. Expand your definition of Love. It is broader and deeper than you can imagine. Love plays with you. Love has magic in it to surprise you. Love creates coincidences to open you up. It is truly magical, and you need to be open to the magic of Love, the surprise, the wonder. Love seeks to appeal to the part of you that re-members this magic—the childlike you. Love asks you to become like a child and spend time re-membering those magical moments of coincidence with wonder and laughter. Be sure to state your coincidence intent and then keep yourselves open to the magic that will follow when you least expect it.

## A Coincidence Intent Technique

*State your intent to receive coincidences. Say, "I joyfully encourage happenings to occur even beyond my beliefs and expectations."*

## Retraining the DNA

We have heard many of you asking why the genetic tampering still affects you today. This manipulation happened long ago... or did it? Re-member, time does not run in a straight line. Past, present, and future flow concurrently. You exist in the now. At some point in time, the genetic manipulation is still occurring. It has become a reality of your three-dimensional world. The manipulation is part of your cellular memory. The cells of your body are like computer chips, and your soul or spark of Creator is the power source. The cellular memory of having only two strands of DNA is within the cells.

"Spirits-in-biology" such as you were created to work together. Your cells act like miniature Askashic Records. The experiences of your lifetimes are stored there. When you are in a life situation that you have experienced before, it triggers a response at the cellular level. The cells release information to the unconscious brain, allowing you to work through the situation more easily.

We also hear you ask how you can repair your damaged DNA. Many of you already have! Like animals who adapt to their surroundings, you have adapted to two strands of DNA like a chameleon that changes its colors to those of its surroundings. Just by reading these words and pursuing other forms of enlightenment, you have started reconnecting. You have heard about people who have had severe brain damage and trained the other parts of the brain to compensate for the loss. This essentially is what has happened with your DNA. By living your life lessons, gathering knowledge, and seeking enlightenment, many of you have retrained your DNA.

Re-member, everything you learn is encoded within your cells. When you re-member your connection to Spirit, it becomes part of your cellular memory. When biology is activated, your cells re-member the Source of Knowledge and make the connection. Many of you have in fact created your

*Driving Without Headlights*

own DNA, rebuilding your own connection. Already babies are being born with twelve strands of DNA, and some have even more. Your doctors and scientists have already noted this phenomenon. As you reconnect, the veil grows thinner. You are re-membering who you are and recognizing the work you have already done.

## The Heart-Brain Connection

The severing of your DNA made you lose the connection that allows the heart and brain to function as one unit. You became out of sync. You forgot how to make your heart and brain function together. You have done much work in reestablishing the heart-brain connection. For too many years, you functioned only in the ego-aggressive energy. The thinning of the veil has allowed you to start re-connecting with the feminine Love-based energy. We are working on the left hemisphere of your brain, trying to soften it up.

If you could visualize it as we do, the left hemisphere of your brain would look something like cement…like part of a road. Your left brain has been trapped because it has so many resistances. It has been wired into the mass consciousness not to change…to continue resisting the feminine right-brain messages. It chooses to communicate with the right brain only when that serves its own purposes. We will help you heal this left brain.

The left brain and right brain are not functioning as they should because of the integration into the brain of what we call the old structure or grid. This grid has distorted people's thinking. It makes people focus on the product, not the process. It has taken people out of the moment. In other words, it makes you feel it is no longer playing the game that counts (the process), only the winning (the product).

## Left-Brain Inertia

The left brain is geared to fight, and we do not want to fight with it. On a subtle level, it still possesses a sort of survival instinct. It is afraid of the unstructuredness of the right brain and the feminine. It is immature and acts a bit like an adolescent male. This creates the male competition you see around you. Most females do not value competition as much as males do. Females come from a more right-brain perspective. The old structure of the brain has made too many people focus on the goal of winning. It is sort of a left-brain inertia that limits the expansion of the heart. All humans need to reconnect the hemispheres of the brain as well as the brain and the heart.

## A Paradigm Shift

How can you do this? First, you need to recognize what the left brain is leading you to think and do at the moment. Then don't fight it; simply have fun. Don't focus on the goal. Laugh. Enjoy what you are doing at the moment. Never mind if you win or lose. Never mind if you are first or last. Have fun!

You, especially in the Western world, have been brainwashed to focus on an individual winning at all costs. You teach your children to compete as soon as they can walk and talk. They see television programs that feature who is best, strongest, or fastest instead of who is happiest or most considerate. Parents push their children to be the first or the best. When children fail to meet their parents' expectations, they become "down-hearted." Their heart connections suffer. Later, they in turn try to make their own children the best. It is a vicious cycle that must be broken.

When enough people begin to laugh and enjoy themselves instead of trying to beat someone else to the goal, there will be a great paradigm shift to right-brain thinking and right-brain values in everyone.

To make a paradigm shift of thinking from left brain to right brain, you must first become aware of your thoughts. Most people go through their lives almost as sleepwalkers, without realizing what kinds of thoughts they are producing and where those thoughts may lead them. Thoughts are living things! Become aware! Take stock, we tell you. Talk to your children about their thoughts and feelings as well. How does it feel to win? How does it feel to lose? How does it feel to come in second, one inch behind the winner?

Many indigenous people on Earth are much more right-brained in their thinking and their values. They enjoy the race, and they congratulate the winner. But they also know enough to salute all of the participants and make sure that everyone feels like a winner. That is the reason the access doors in their hearts and brains are more widely open to information from beyond the veil. They have not lost their connections.

## The Heart Energy Generator

People on Earth have put the heart on a purely physical level. Yet the heart is actually a dimensional doorway with great power of its own. It is a generator of Love energy, and it accepts different frequencies. It is like the brain of the soul. A direct line goes up from the heart to the physical brain. But there is another line, invisible, which has been put in by the dark cousins—a black line that goes from the brain to the heart and sucks heart energy away.

There is also an energy field around the heart, a magnetic resonance that once helped to create not only Love but also wonderment and magic. There used to be more magic on Earth back in the days when Earth was not so solid. Then the dark cousins arrived and put a magnetic grid around the Earth to enable their spaceships to land. But it also created a roadblock between the hearts and brains of humans on Earth.

## Speed Bumps on the Road to Enlightenment

It prevented the heart from giving and receiving Love as it had done previously.

Although the road has been blocked, the road itself is still there. Individuals who have intent to restore their connections can open it. Just hearing about this roadblock and trying to visualize it will make a difference. Visualization is real and can be used to heal and restore the aspects within you that need healing—as long as you have intent to heal and state your intent with strong feelings.

Seeing the roadblock changes it. It is simpler than anyone thinks. Close your eyes and try to visualize a blockage in the route between your heart and your brain. Make it as real looking as you can. Now visualize the warmth of Love flowing from your heart to dissolve the blockage. By observing blockage such as this and stating your strong intent to remove it, you give your heart the power to change it.

When people begin realizing that the heart is a much larger and more powerful organ than they supposed, they will be able to use the heart's energy to heal it. Allow your heart, your generator of Love, to expand to its full capacity and shine its headlights on your road to enlightenment. Your heart is waiting for this to happen.

*Driving Without Headlights*

## Speed Bumps on the Road to Enlightenment

Pain is surmounted
With help from above;
All is forgiven
With expressions of Love;
And so it is healed...

CHAPTER **4**

# Life Lessons: When Speed Bumps Become Roadblocks

You come into life dressed for the part. Your human biology is the first layer, masking who you really are. Unlike the grand Shakespearian plays, you do not get a dress rehearsal. Instead, you stumble onto the stage of life with no clear idea of the plot or motive. Just when you think you know who all the characters are, someone new enters the stage and confuses you with a completely new dialogue. Life is a comedy of errors, many of which contain no humor.

With a vague sense of purpose and a trunk full of costumes, you take your act out on the road to enlightenment. The road may be short and never go beyond your local theater, or it may be a wild ride with stages all over the world. But no matter where the road leads, you are always the star.

## Karmic Speed Bumps

Karma has determined the costumes you wear each lifetime. As you interact with your fellow players and work through the plot, you are able to shed your heavy costume, eventually allowing your true essence to emerge. It is important to re-member that whether you have the starring role as the good guy or the bad guy, you are all the same underneath the costumes.

In Chapter 2, we discussed life choices, contract agreements, and the role that karma plays in them. In this chapter, we will discuss how to get over these karmic speed bumps. Your life lessons are what enable you to break the karmic cycle. The master key to working through your life lessons is simply Love. But we hear you say Love is no simple thing. You ask how we can Love someone who has hurt us and how we can Love ourselves when we have done harm. Our response is this: re-member. Look beneath the costume. Re-member who you and your fellow actors truly are.

## Forgiving Others

The key to unlocking the floodgate of Love is forgiveness. Forgiveness is the biggest speed bump that you will ever encounter. In fact, for some people, forgiveness turns into a roadblock they never get past. Many speed bumps in life require Love and forgiveness in order for you to overcome them. When you do not overcome them, the same lesson will be played out over several lifetimes until you do. Many of you on Earth at this time have already ended your karmic bonds. You are here assisting others to release their hold on anger, hate, and resentment.

On the other hand, many of you wrap these negative emotions around you like a cloak. You have held onto them for so long that they have hardened your hearts. These negative emotions are the legacy of the dark cousins. Before they came

## *Life Lessons: When Speed Bumps Become Roadblocks*

to your lovely planet, there was no need for these emotions. There was no murder, no abuse, no greed, and no illness. These things are what the dark cousins instigated, and the negative emotions are the byproducts.

The key to allowing forgiveness to work in your life is to re-member. Allow the memories of Home to come through so that you can see the bigger picture of the situation. There is a saying on your planet that is more important than you know. It is, "look for the silver lining," the shining light inside you all.

When you are in an abusive life situation with someone, whether a family member, a friend, or a spouse, you need to find that spark of good, that piece of who he or she really is, and focus on it—that one moment when he or she can allow the corner of the veil to lift and let a tiny bit of his or her true self shine on you. It is extremely difficult to forgive abuse and pain, but your saving grace is to re-member that you asked for it. You and the abusing party agreed to this lesson. In the depth of your own pain, it is nearly impossible to see the pain inside him or her for having to inflict it upon you.

So when you are on your road to enlightenment, and you come to the speed bump of forgiveness, you need to search your heart for that one brief glimpse of who the abuser really is. There may only be one or there may be many glimpses, but they come fast so as not to ruin the lesson for you. It can be a word, a gesture, or only a glimmer in his or her eye, but sometime in that relationship, it will appear and be the foundation for forgiveness.

Do not confuse forgiveness with allowing the abuse to continue. Just because you accept that the situation was orchestrated between you does not mean you have to stay in the relationship. You bless it and move on. It does not serve you to stay in an endless cycle of abuse, even if you know from where it came. Often, forgiveness can only be achieved through distance. You need to use the knowledge gained and grow from there.

## Forgiving Yourself

An abusive relationship is only one example of the many situations that may need forgiveness in your life. Not only do you need to forgive others, you need to forgive and Love yourself. Situations will often occur when, due to negative emotions, you unintentionally cause someone pain. Acknowledging that these emotions are not who you really are, and that you have free will to choose another path of expression, allows you to be able to forgive yourself.

How do you forgive yourself when you intentionally harm or kill someone? Look at the word "intentionally." If you break it down, you will find that you end up with the root word "intent." Perhaps the intent was part of your contract for this lifetime. You need to think of this event within the grand design of all things. If you express true remorse for this deed, you have accomplished your half of the lesson. Those of you who do not express remorse will continue in the karmic cycle.

## Guilt

Guilt is another huge speed bump on your road to enlightenment. There is usually some tangible evidence in your life for the origin of the guilt you are feeling. But many of you wear layers of guilt not of your making. You feel guilty about things for which you were not, and are not, responsible. Children who have been abused and women who have been raped often feel responsible for the things that have been inflicted upon them. There seems to be no basis in their lives for why they should feel this way. Therein lies the key—there is no basis in this life. What you are experiencing is cellular memory brought on by the trauma. Re-member the karmic pattern—if you were the abuser in one life, you may become the abused in the next.

*Life Lessons: When Speed Bumps Become Roadblocks*

You have noticed that not all people who are abused feel guilty. These were able to forgive themselves in the previous life. When you acknowledge the guilt and tell yourself it was not your fault, you release the guilt's karmic pattern.

## Fears

Fears are another speed bump. People who carry many fears are usually souls who have not been incarnated many times. The veil is thick, and they often feel alone and abandoned. They do not re-member their connection. Fear of dying is usually the greatest of them all. For those of you who have been around the block a few times, the reverse is true—you cannot wait to go Home. You re-member the beauty of Home. However, even highly evolved souls can have fears. They, too, are often generated by cellular memory.

We mentioned in a previous chapter that cataclysmic events could cause sudden death. For example, many of you who were on Atlantis have fears of water and bridges. Many who were killed by the Nazis in the gas chambers have claustrophobia. Cellular memory not only triggers fear, it also manifests itself in illnesses. Asthma is common among people who reincarnated after dying in the gas chambers. Often an illness or complaint will come on all of a sudden when you reach a certain age.

Say you were shot in the leg by a Civil War bullet at age 23. In this lifetime, at age 23, you might suddenly experience an unexplained pain in the same leg. There have been many cases like this documented by hypnotists during past life regressions. Regressions are a wonderful tool in releasing these stuck emotions and opening your heart. You may also release these emotions on your own without a facilitator. We will talk more about fears in Chapter 10.

*Speed Bumps on the Road to Enlightenment*

## Metaphysical Heart Bypass

In order to release these emotions and any other negative feelings you may have, you need to open your heart to Love. As discussed in Chapter 3, most people's hearts were blocked long ago when the dark cousins disconnected the road from the brain to the heart. In Chapter 3, you were instructed how to open this blockage by visualization and stating aloud your intent to heal. There is always more than one way to heal broken or disconnected parts.

The other effective method is called the metaphysical heart bypass. You can perform it by sending your Love energy out to others: to children, to animals, to friends and neighbors, and to people in need. But you must do more than merely think it. You must actually do it by interacting lovingly with the people and animals you Love. They will soon reciprocate with their own Love energy, which really gets a two-way flow going.

Love energy is also created when you show appreciation for natural beauty. Go out into the natural environment and open your heart to the view of a sunset, the mountains, trees and flowers, flowing water, a starlit night. Stand with your feet planted firmly on the ground. If your heart is truly open, you can feel the Love energy engulfing you. It may even bring tears to your eyes.

## Changing Your "Dwelling Place"

Now that you know what Love feels like, become aware of what else creates this feeling within you: the presence of a loved one, joyous laughter, sharing precious moments, the giving of yourself unconditionally when you help others. Doesn't it feel good inside when you do these things? It is the feeling of Love.

You need to realize that your previous perspectives have been skewed. When you shift to a new perspective,

*Life Lessons: When Speed Bumps Become Roadblocks*

what you are doing is changing your dwelling place. For most people, their dwelling place has been in their brains, not their hearts. The roadblocks to the heart have made people unaware and trapped in this other dwelling place. In order to shift perspective, many people need, first, to heal the unwanted things in their dwelling places.

## Releasing Judgments

The unspoken voices within you that have been blocking the opening of your heart need to be heard before they leave. Theirs is not just a magic disappearing act. These voices are real. These voices are judgments—judgments from other people, judgments from your religion, judgments from society at large, but also judgments put in by you about yourself. You may never have articulated these judgments before, but try it and see what happens.

When you allow your voices of judgment to be heard, then they can be released. What will they say? Perhaps things like, "My brain knows much more than my heart," or, "The brain knows better how a person should behave than the heart does," or, "I would lose control if I left my behavior up to my heart," or, "If I open my heart, I will only get hurt again."

Listen to your own voices. You may want to make a list of your judgments against the opening of your heart. Once you start listing judgments, you will be surprised by the number you have held almost secretly since you were a child. Once these inner voices of judgment have had their say, then you can begin releasing them one by one. How? Try speaking aloud your release of each of these judgments. Be sincere. Say the judgment releases more than once if it helps to make them genuine. Use emotion. Let your feelings out.

Here are some judgment releases you can try. Not all of these judgments may apply to you. Read them over, and concentrate on the ones that resonate within your heart. If you listen, your heart will let you know what it needs.

- I release the judgment that my brain knows much more than my heart does.
- I release the judgment that my brain knows better how I should behave than my heart does.
- I release the judgment that brains are more down-to-Earth and hearts are too flighty and emotional.
- I release the judgment that I would lose control if I left my behavior up to my heart.
- I release the judgment that if I open my heart, I will only get hurt again.

The releasing of these judgments can sometimes trigger some heavy emotional responses within you. If you are moved to tears, then let them flow. Do not be afraid of these emotions. They are your healing.

## Using Intuition

Now what happens? First, each judgment release will allow the heart to expand. You need to stay open in this heart area. Try not to get angry. Try not to worry about things as you have in the past. Allow Love to begin its process of healing. How will you know how to behave if you do not listen to your brain as you have in the past? Use your intuition, which guides you from your heart. Listen for "the still small voice." Try following your intuition. It will not guide you falsely.

Intuition operates through feelings. Once you are aware of it, you will be able to feel what is right and what is wrong when you are faced with challenges. Ask yourself what you should do in a certain situation, and then feel for the answer. If you do not accept the strongest feeling for what you should do, then you will begin to feel anxious and uncomfortable. You will need to change your direction in order to feel better about it. If you prefer not to follow an inner feeling again and again, it will lose its power to guide you.

But if you do choose to live intuitively, then the right doors will open for you, both figuratively and literally. Coincidences that seem incredible will happen in your life, as we discussed in Chapter 3. As you learned, they are signposts from your higher self that you are going in the right direction—that you are "in sync," that your headlights are finally ready to light the road you must follow.

## Start the Process

Spirit has wanted to get onto this planet for a long, long time. The forces of control from the days of the dark star cousins have been blocking the magnetic resonance around the hearts of people. But as Love begins to process people's judgment releases from their hearts, the brain itself is going to soften up and allow Love to enter.

All you need to do is to start the process. Your heart knows what to do once the judgments against it are released. Although invisible, this process is something real, something more important than anyone can imagine. The grid around the Earth, which was put there to create its gravity and density, will actually change. A new evolution of Spirit will occur.

Then, when you stand before one of the large roadblocks we have mentioned and you can find no way to get around or over it, look for the silver lining. Get to the heart and soul of the matter, and you will find that the roadblock does not really exist. It is but a mirage. When you encounter the smaller speed bumps, use your discernment to see if they are truly speed bumps or if they are merely stumbling blocks placed by your guides to keep you true to your map. If you use your intuition, you will know.

## Apathy

You may think that hate, fear, anger, lust, and resentment are the worst of the negative emotions, the biggest of the speed bumps on your road to enlightenment. They are not. One emotion enables all the others to occur—apathy. In fact, apathy is not really an emotion at all. It is the lack of emotion. The severing of your DNA and heart connections made you apathetic. You became like drones so that the dark cousins could manipulate you.

Many of the dark star cultures operated from a "hive mentality," like bees and ants. All thoughts and directions came from one source. Being able to think and feel as individuals were things with which they were not familiar. Due to this unfamiliarity with feelings, they underestimated the effectiveness of their control of you over a long period. They did not realize that the living example of your intent was under your very feet—Mother Earth.

The vibrations of Love coming through the soles of your feet became the first tendrils reconnecting your emotions after they had been severed. You have all heard the expression, "the eyes are the windows of the soul." Even in your apathetic state, what did you see before you? It was nature. Mother Nature displayed herself before you in all her glorious beauty. The beauty of nature resonates with the Love vibrations. Mother Earth has always been there for you. She has maintained the balance for eons. But in your apathy, you have caused her much pain. Now is the time to shake off the remnants of this lack of feeling and support her. Here is what she has to say to you.

*Life Lessons: When Speed Bumps Become Roadblocks*

## Step into Your Future

Take heed, Children of Earth, this is your Mother speaking! You need to know that some action is required of you. You are not fine just as you are! Not just mankind, but the whole Earth, is at a critical mass! Right now! Today! This moment! Now is the time to take the most critical action of all—stepping into your future. Either you are going to step into your future as a peaceful and enlightened society, or you will fall back and have to do it all over again.

Don't you re-member? The Earth and her people have arrived at this very moment many times before. Erase your apathy! Open your memory banks! Think about Lemuria! Atlantis! The Great Flood! Awaken, Children of Earth! Your words, thoughts, and actions of today are the blueprints for tomorrow.

Are you waiting to see what 2012 A.D. will bring? 2012 is the year that astrological cycles are completed, the year that the Mayan calendar ends, the year that indigenous people around the globe say a new world will be born. By then, it will be too late.

If you wait to see what is going to happen, the future will take care of itself. It will be out of your hands. You will be in for a rough ride not to your liking. Think about how you buy a lottery ticket. If you wait to see what the first number will turn out to be before buying your ticket, it will be too late, because the machines will have been shut off.

## Do Not Be a Fence Sitter

We join Mother Nature with our own appeal—take action now! Do not be a fence sitter! We want to shake you up! Step off the fence! Take a leap of faith! If you do not step into it and create your future, you will re-create your past!

How will you do it? How does one create the future? Look around you, and you will see. Something needs healing besides you. Haven't you noticed? It is Mother Earth. She is hurting. She may be dying. This great planet that has supported your life for millennia is calling out for your help. She is shaking the ground beneath the feet of many. She is flashing lightning in the skies, skewing her weather this way and that, parading tornadoes across the land and hurricanes across the ocean to rip up anything in front of them. Is this the way a mother acts toward her children? Only in an emergency. Only to get their attention.

Don't you see what is happening? To the rivers and oceans? To the birds and animals? To the rain forests? Where are all the strange new diseases and epidemics coming from? Are you observing it only from the safety of your living room in front of the television? What will you do when the electricity goes off—for good? When all the batteries finally run down? By then, it will be too late. Children of Earth, shake off your apathy! Pay attention to your planet! You already did Atlantis. The people there waited too long. You do not want to do that again.

## Earth, a Reflection of Her People

What you may not realize is the kind of connection you have with the Earth. You are all part of the same energy. The Earth is alive just as you are. If you allow the Earth to die, you will die also. Can that happen? It already has in the past. You are a reflection of the Earth's life cycle. Whenever the Earth has eruptions, there is always war among her human inhabitants, because you mirror one another.

Great upheavals have nearly shaken the Earth to death in the past. Whenever there have been massive Earth changes, there has been great violence among the people. The Earth herself tries to maintain a balance between upheaval and calm

*Life Lessons: When Speed Bumps Become Roadblocks*

by using her waters—her healing waters. Great floods of the past were not a negative thing. They were a calming, soothing response to the violence—a healing balm. You must respect your bodies of water: the rivers, lakes, and oceans. They are the healing ointment for Earth.

You are experiencing more rain in areas that never before had so much in order to calm and soothe the Earth from the violence in other parts of the world. High water and flooding tell people to step back and give nature some room. You are living in flood plains and on barrier islands that were never intended for people's dwellings. Excess rains also wash the land of fertilizers and pollutants, making it whole again.

## Show You Care for the Earth

You must show you care for the Earth. If you do not allow nature a future, then you will not have a future yourselves. If you do not allow nature to survive, then you will not survive. What about the extraterrestrials, you hear some people asking? Won't they save us if we go too far with things like our weapons of mass destruction? The extraterrestrials are stepping back to see what Earth people themselves are going to do. If they have to step in and save the Earth, they will be saving it for themselves, not for you.

Think of how many times humans have been given this opportunity before and they blew it. There is greater potential for disaster on Earth now because there are more people here than ever before— people who need to wake up. But, due to your mass communications, there is more potential to wake them up than ever before.

*Speed Bumps on the Road to Enlightenment*

## Speak Out for the Earth

The potential is here for a wonderful future, but you must reach out and take it. You must make the effort, like reaching for the brass ring on the merry-go-round. Don't let it go around again. Now is the time to act. By acting, we mean speaking out:

- Tell others what is happening.
- Say aloud for everyone to hear how you must all act together in light of this emergency.
- Ask the Creator in your prayers to help you do the right thing and say the right thing.
- Speak aloud your convictions about saving the Earth.
- If you are going to hug a tree, make sure someone sees you do it, and then tell him or her why!

## A Cosmic Zing

This chapter is our celestial slap in the face for you! Hello! Wake up! Eradicate your apathy! We see so many of you in a daze, almost a hypnotic trance. You have been waiting so long for something awesome to happen that you are almost catatonic from the waiting. So many of you came into this life for this very time, and now the time is here. But you don't recognize it. You have been waiting for something complicated, such as a sign telling you to step into your contract and do your part. Everyone seems to be looking for that big cosmic zing.

It is already here. It has been here all along. It is an everyday thing. It is this life you are living—loving your neighbor, recycling, not trashing your environment. Wake up and claim it. If you have strong convictions about Earth matters, don't keep them to yourself. Voice it. It has to be spoken. It has to be shared. If you feel strongly about recycling and you see someone throwing out a bottle, talk to him or her about it. Talk about the toxins in the atmosphere and the pollutants in the water.

## Making a Difference

If you have a conviction, you need to share it. You cannot just feel sorry about it. Not saying anything is like casting a negative vote for the future. You don't have to be an extremist to speak out. Speaking to one person at a time may be planting a seed that will cause a chain reaction. But if you don't step into your future like this, it's not going to be there.

How can one person make a difference, you wonder. One person is the most important part of the picture. Although you are separate individuals, you have inner connections with everyone else. What you feel within yourself affects others. What you say aloud becomes a part of them also. The "hundredth monkey effect" is real. When more than fifty percent of the planet's inhabitants show their concern for one another and the Earth, a great shift in consciousness will occur.

## The Time Is Now

The time is now. Some of you are holding back, believing that your children are your future. You are nurturing your children but not the Earth, because you think that your children will take care of it. You won't have to bother. We say, if you don't put your own energy into preserving the Earth, there will be no Earth for which your children can become caretakers. The time is now.

You are the Children of the Universe. That's you! Wake up and smell the flowers! If you don't say anything to the person who throws a piece of trash or dumps garbage into the lake, you become that person. You must step beyond the "I am"

*Speed Bumps on the Road to Enlightenment*

singular, which is selfish, and become the "we are" plural. Only when you finally become plural can all of you truly become singular, with one heart. That is how you will step into the future—along a highway with no roadblocks.

## Judgment Release Technique

Make a list of your judgments. Say aloud and mean it, "I release…." Do this with each judgment.

*Life Lessons: When Speed Bumps Become Roadblocks*

*Speed Bumps on the Road to Enlightenment*

Left or right,

From above or below,

All is correct

Which ever way you go;

And so it is learned…

CHAPTER 5

# Detours: If You Drive Off The Road, Can You Get Back On?

The roads of life are many and varied. Some of you stay in the slow lane, going through life at a steady pace, caught up in your own private world. The honking horns and speeding passers-by are but a moment of annoyance for you. Then suddenly before you looms a blinking sign: ROAD CLOSED—DETOUR. You find yourself in strange new territory. These detours can present themselves in many ways—dramatically or joyously. Whatever the circumstances, they change the routine of your mundane life. These detours are things that cannot be ignored. Whether you consciously want it to or not, your life is going to change.

You ask if you can ever get back on your original route. We say you never really leave it. These detours are the entrance ramps to your contracts. They lead you into the relationships and circumstances for your chosen life lessons. No road taken is ever wrong. As with any detour, you follow the signs and look for the new set of rules that apply to the situation in which you find yourself.

Some of you can follow the signs with ease. In a short period, you have navigated yourself back to your comfort zone. But for many of you, the signs become confusing. You find yourself going around in circles. Long periods go by, and you still seem to be lost within the situation. Eventually, you find a road parallel to the one on which you were originally. It may be a little bumpier, a little faster, or slower than you want to go, but you find that you are able to navigate it.

## Illness or Disability

Illness or a disability can be one of these detours. Suddenly, you may find yourself unable to manage even the simplest things for yourself. You may feel like you are a burden to your caretakers. But life lessons, like time, run in more than one direction. As important as it is to help another person, it is equally as important to receive help yourself graciously. Even though you may not be able to drive the car by yourself, it does not mean that you cannot enjoy the ride. Once you accept your physical limitations, there is no room for self-pity and anger. Love fills the empty spaces.

The key word here is *accept*. First, you need to accept the situation. This does not mean that you accept everything the doctor tells you. After a car accident, if you are told that you will never be able to walk again, or never be able to use your hands again, or never be able to see again, what you accept is the situation, not someone else's opinion of the outcome. You, and not the doctor, are still in charge of yourself and the outcome. To accept a negative evaluation may steer you in the direction of a self-fulfilling prophecy. In other words, if you believe you cannot be cured, you will not be.

*If You Drive Off The Road, Can You Get Back On?*

## Affecting the Outcome

On the other hand, there are many ways you can positively affect the outcome if you accept the situation. You can contact a variety of therapists and try different therapies. You can talk with others who have been in the same situation and follow their advice if it seems appropriate. You can research possible cures in libraries or on the internet. Modern medical techniques can perform miracles. So can meditation and prayer. Set up a regimen of any of these treatments, and follow it until it brings some results. Keep your mind and heart open and your attitude toward yourself a positive one. Even if you find that these therapies offer no help, you should not give up on life. Just look for the new set of rules that apply to your situation. Having physical limitations does not mean that you cannot lead a happy life.

Secondly, you must accept help from others. Friends, family, and loved ones have positive Love energy to give you. Too many people who have always been in charge of their lives often find it difficult to be in a so-called "helpless" situation where they must accept help from those around them. You need to re-member that this whole situation may be a karmic one, where others are returning the assistance that you once gave to them. Accept it with thanks, and let its positive energy infuse your being. Turning away freely offered help might delay or even prevent your cure. Re-member, the people who are trying to help you may be fulfilling their contracts, too.

## Grief

Grief is a huge detour. All of you go down this road. Death is not the only thing that you grieve. Many things can leave you with an overwhelming sense of loss. That is what grief is—a sense of loss. Grief strikes you so deeply because grief is felt at a cellular level. The feelings of disconnection and separation have been a part of you since the arrival of the dark cousins.

## Speed Bumps on the Road to Enlightenment

At a cellular level, you still feel the severing of your ties with Mother Earth. How can you grieve the loss of your connection to Mother Earth, you ask, if you don't even re-member it?

The imprint of your cells re-members your connection to all things. At some point, you all experience some kind of sadness and grief for which you can find no basis. It comes from deep inside and washes over you like a cloudburst out of a seemingly clear sky. In times of quiet solitude, you open yourself up to the world around you, most especially the world underneath your feet. Mother Earth re-members your connection to her. Her grief and love for you are constant and always surround you. When you are in those quiet moments and your guard is down, the emanating emotions from Mother Earth are felt. The spark of recognition is lit, and you respond.

Grief is also the trigger for the onset of many negative emotions on the Earth plane. How many of you, in your grief, have cursed God? How many of you have expressed fear, hate, anger, or resentment towards the person or thing that caused the separation?

The negative aspects of your Earth life began with your separation from Mother Earth. Grief and negative emotions have a common bond. Even those of you who do not flounder in the negative emotions feel grief just as strongly. Logically, you know the reason for the separation and that you will be together again someday when this life ultimately ends. But no matter what your intellect tells you, your heart only feels loss.

## Grief in the Higher Realms

Grief is not exclusive to mankind alone. It is felt even in the higher realms, for grief is actually the highest expression of Love. When you enter into life and leave your soul family behind, they mourn the loss of your company. Even though contact is periodically shared in the dream state, all sorely miss

*If You Drive Off The Road, Can You Get Back On?*

the brilliance of your light. When you express grief (the louder and more tear-filled, the better), you create more space within you to hold Love. When you create more room for Love, you also create space for new people, places, and adventures. After a period of grieving, you may find that your life is busier than before and that you are traveling in the fast lane. However, since you never get over loving a person, you always carry an aspect of that grief within you.

## Helping

But what if you cannot stop grieving or crying? What if your period of grieving shows no signs of ending, and you feel you cannot go on with your life? You must then take positive action to open the doorway of your heart. One of the most effective ways to start this process is by helping someone else. Assist someone else in need. If you do not know of anyone, volunteer to work in a children's program. Volunteer to visit residents in a nursing home. Become a foster parent. Read stories to children at the public library. Be a driver for Meals on Wheels. Pick up trash along the highway. Ask the Red Cross how you can help. As you begin to focus away from yourself and your own grief, toward others and their needs, you will feel the sorrowful feelings within you begin to abate. You will feel the doorway to your heart begin to open to receive Love.

## Be Happy

Focus on being happy. Look for little things to make you happy. When you see the people you are helping becoming happy, you should feel that way, too. Focusing on happiness builds upon itself, bringing even more joy into your life. Once the doorway to your heart begins opening to the Love vibration of happiness, it is difficult for negative situations to close it completely again.

## Give Compliments

Another key that unlocks the doorway to Love is giving compliments. When you see someone wearing clothing or jewelry you admire, tell them. When you see someone helping another, tell him or her. When someone smiles at you, tell him or her how good it makes you feel. Surely, such a simple thing as giving a compliment cannot really affect you, can it? Yes, it is quite true. An invisible light actually bounces back and forth between two people when compliments are exchanged. Although some people have trouble receiving compliments when they have been hurt, a sincere compliment contains the light of compassion. It can truly have an effect on a closed door where the hurt is.

Give yourself a compliment as well. Have you ever done "mirror work"? Simply paste a post-it note to yourself on your mirror, saying something such as, "You Look Wonderful Today!" or, "I Love Your Smile!" or, "You Are Great!" These notes will make you stand up, take notice whenever you look in the mirror, and see yourself looking back with this message for you.

## Repetition and Laughter

Do you think these messages are not sincere? Keep looking and reading and saying them aloud, and eventually repetition helps them to sink in. Whether you wrote them for fun or for self-esteem, even a joke brings laughter. And laughter starts Love flowing. It's true. Try it and see. Keep the notes posted for as long as they get your attention. You need to re-member that repetition is another key to the door-opening process.

When you change your calendar each month, change your notes of encouragement. In any given month, there are memories of events that have caused some kind of emotional response in you. Use your positive, uplifting, or humorous affirmations to help you over these emotional speed bumps.

*If You Drive Off The Road, Can You Get Back On?*

## Observe and Reflect on Your Feelings

Can you feel your doorway beginning to creak open? Observing how you feel is still another door opener. We have a saying that reminds us how "observation brings evolution." It is important to observe how you feel within your body after you have begun helping others, being happy, giving compliments, and laughing. What makes you feel good? Does anything still make you feel bad?

Reflecting on your observations gives acknowledgement to your senses that you are aware of what is going on within you. As we have mentioned previously, too many people on the planet are sleepwalking. They do not realize their doorways are closed, and they are cut off from Love and the Creator. They need to begin the door-opening process by observing their feelings and reflecting on them.

## Observe With Closed Eyes

One of the brain's functions is to observe. This observation alone will help the heart begin to heal. It will signal the heart that adjustments may be needed—that balance, mending, and healing may be necessary. Then you will be ready to open your grieving heart to Love.

How are you doing this observation? With your eyes? With your body? With your heart? You need to know that the eyes in your head are laden with judgments. Even the muscles of the eyes are infiltrated by a judgment system that labels what you physically see with words such as "good" or "bad," "like" or "dislike," "friendly" or "untrustworthy," or "not interesting." You will know if such judgments are a part of your assessments when you observe. A better observation process for opening doorways involves closing your eyes and feeling in your body what something is like.

## Whole Feeling

Whole feeling is another gift that was taken away from you. Everything That Is can be felt with all your senses. Only in the smallest of degrees are you still able to do this. When listening to music, you might say, "This sounds harsh...or soft...or mellow." You are experiencing it with more than your hearing. You are giving it dimension. Re-member, there are many dimensions to All Things. You already know you can hear music, and you can feel its beat or vibration. But did you know that music can also be seen and tasted?

Everything has a separate vibration. All vibrations have a sound. All sounds have a color, all color has a smell, and all smell produces a taste. Each vibration you encounter will be felt by you differently than by someone who may be standing right next to you.

Why is this, you ask? Because you vibrate, too. When other vibrations enter your vibrational field, they mingle and bounce off one another. This provides you with variety. When new frequencies enter your vibrational circle, they create their own blends. These co-minglings of vibrations give you your personal likes and dislikes.

Sometimes, when you first meet someone, you instantly don't like him or her. This is a result of your vibrations finding it difficult to blend. As you spend time with that person, you can often become good friends because your vibrations have found their common pattern or rhythm. A few people, like some foods or music, may never be to your liking during this lifetime. Do not let your first impressions form your judgments for you. Allow yourself the opportunity to *feel* out the situation.

*If You Drive Off The Road, Can You Get Back On?*

## Compassion

Have compassion for other persons and for yourself. Compassion is another key to opening the doorway to your heart. Everyone on the Earth plane in a human body who is not vibrating at the speed of light has blockages to the heart. In the future, we will have "feeling tanks" where groups of people can come together to resolve negative situations by feeling together, much like today's "think tanks" where intellectual problems are solved by thinking together. It all begins with observation. If you can observe yourself, then you know that your heart, not your brain, is in control. And the doorway opens.

## Visualization

Try to visualize what to do or which way to go. Try one way and then another. Try to feel what you hear or what your body says, not just what your eyes see. Visualization itself is another heart door opener. Can you imagine what a doorway to your heart looks like? Can you visualize opening it? Perhaps it is stuck shut. Close your eyes, and try visualizing what this door to your heart looks like. If it looks plain, cold, or hard, this may be a reflection of how you feel about your heart. But you can change it by visualizing a beautifully ornate door. There is no lock, so you don't need a key. It is your intent that opens this door.

## Intent

How will you use intent to open the door? One simple way is to speak your intent aloud with as much emotion as you can muster—"I intend for the doorway in my heart to open!" Say it repeatedly until you feel something. Do not be surprised if the doorway opens and buried emotions flood out. Go with the flow. Cry. Shed tears of anguish at being trapped for so long,

*Speed Bumps on the Road to Enlightenment*

and then asked to be healed. Say it aloud. Have strong intent for Love to heal you. Let the tears of anguish turn into tears of relief.

"I, Janice, have to interrupt here to say that I try all of the techniques that have been given to us. When I said very loudly, three or four times, 'I intend for the doorway in my heart to open,' I was surprised to note that something did happen. I could feel something rise up and get stuck in my throat, like a lump in my throat. Then I felt tears of relief ready to flow, so I cried, and I immediately felt better."

Intention techniques like this are heart door openers. Intentions you put out such as this return to you faster today than ever before. Be sure when you speak out your intentions that you also include your intent to heal, or your doorway may get jammed again. Using your intent like this dissolves the door and creates an open portal into which Love can continuously flow. Once your heart's doorway is open, you are off your detour and back on the road to enlightenment.

### Roadmaps to Your Heart's Doorway

- *Help others.*
- *Be happy.*
- *Give compliments.*
- *Laugh.*
- *Observe how you feel.*
- *Reflect on your observations.*
- *Experience whole feeling.*
- *Have compassion for others.*
- *Visualize what to do.*
- *Speak your intent aloud with emotion.*

*If You Drive Off The Road, Can You Get Back On?*

## Relationships

*Relationships* are yet another detour. You come into life within a group of souls that start you on your journey. But as you travel down the road of life, many people join you for the ride: friends, lovers, children. These relationships are the Route 66 of your life lesson. They present you with rest stops, historical markers, scenic views, and strangely wondrous attractions. There are positive relationships and seemingly negative relationships. Re-member, all are beneficial to your life's lessons. Always bless the bad along with the good.

## Children

A long detour for many people involves their children. You need to listen to young children. They have not been corrupted by the Earth distortions during their early years as you were. They can show you truths and teach you things you need to know. Yes, you can learn from your children. They are not blank slates, for they have been here before and are now coming back directly from the higher regions.

Unfortunately, many of you treat your children with disregard. You do not recognize them as the wise souls that they are. Instead, you need to realize that children are worthy individuals who should be treated with respect. Although they may be smaller and require your care, they are wise souls returning to Earth to bring the Creator's Love with them. Your job is to see that they grow up in a safe, healthy, loving environment where they are treated with respect and learn to treat others the same.

## Generational Patterns of Treatment

Many parents of today were in some ways mistreated by their own parents. Even if they were not, they can look around them and see many friends and acquaintances with stories of bad childhoods. Physical abuse, verbal abuse, sexual abuse, and neglect against their children can run through families for generations as though it was genetically programmed. When parents treat their children harshly, they need to know they are not operating out of choice but from their generational patterns. If they think about it and step back to observe how they are now treating their own children in the same manner, they will not want to do what they are doing.

Most parents do not know how to cope because their attention is on so many other things these days. They need to stop right now and reflect on how they are treating their children. They need to take down the walls they put up when they were a child that, in effect, limited their expression and the expansion of their hearts. Harsh discipline was done in the name of "control." Parents felt that if they did not control their children's behavior, chaos would result. Thus, they often used ridicule as a weapon of enforcement. Are you still using it? Fear of ridicule may still permeate your own life. Does it?

## Your "Child-Self"

Parents of today need to heal the part of them that still feels the way they were ridiculed as a child. They need to look at their own children and listen to them. It is a world into which they can actually step. If they do step into their children's world consciously, they may be able to heal their own "child-self" that still holds memories of being ill-treated. Such an action may have a surprising effect on the parents' present lives. This eye-opening experience may make them decide to change their routines, to change their desire to control their children's lives, even to expand their own lives, bringing in more fun and Love.

*If You Drive Off The Road, Can You Get Back On?*

Many parents still have anger against their own parents for being mistreated. This feeling is often reflected in their relationships. When they deal with their children in a more open, loving manner, it will help to heal the earlier "child-self" of theirs that was so injured by their parents. Some readers may be more familiar with the term "inner child" than "child-self." We use the term "child-self," because it represents a person outside of the parent whom they can talk to and play with as they do their own children. Many people are still busy protecting this child-self and don't even know it.

## Love Yourself

Love who you are. Do not let someone else's judgments rule your life. With your eyes free of judgments, look in a mirror and love the angel/child staring back at you. Loving yourself will enable you to break the patterns. It is possible to break the generational patterns of abuse. It only takes one person— you. Simply turn on your directional signal and change lanes.

## Healing Regret, Remorse, and Rage

For people who have regret and remorse about things they may have already done to their children, they need to make a decision right now to start out new and do things differently. As they choose to do it differently with their children, they need to use prayer, intent, and Love to help them view their earlier child-self and the abuse it suffered. Then that abuse can stop controlling their lives. They should have intent that the Light of Love step in and heal the effects of the abuse. When rage comes up at the person who affected their lives in this manner, Spirit wants to hear their rage and bring Love into it. When it is healed, a wondrous expansion will take place on all levels of a person's existence, going back through generations. And another roadblock will be overcome.

## Visualize Loving Light

Many people believe they have to heal themselves before they present themselves to the Creator. This is not the case. Creator wants to help them with this healing. You can bring the Light of Love into your body by closing your eyes and visualizing this Loving Light coming down into your body through the top of your head, behind your eyes, down through your throat, through your heart, through your solar plexus, through your genitals, and down through the base of your spine and into the Earth.

Take your time with this visualization, stopping at each of these energy centers, and allowing the Loving Light to penetrate and heal. Can you feel it? All the better. Do this exercise every day until you feel yourself becoming lighter and happier. Breathe deeply at the same time, taking in breath through your nose, holding it, and releasing it through your mouth.

## Loving Light Healing Technique

- *Close your eyes and visualize Loving Light coming down in a stream into your body. (Even a pinhead of light is enough)*

- *Visualize this light stopping to penetrate and heal each energy center (top of head, behind eyes, down throat, through heart, through solar plexus, through genitals, through base of spine, into the Earth).*

- *At the same time, breathe deeply through your nose; hold it; release through your mouth.*

- *Do this exercise daily until you feel lighter and happier.*

*If You Drive Off The Road, Can You Get Back On?*

## Wrong Perceptions

We have heard you ask how a road filled with crime and violence can be the right road. We still say there are no wrong roads. Life is like a ten-lane highway where the different lanes represent negative and positive aspects. The road winds through time, and the lanes cross over as they do in construction areas. You may be in a violent lane now, but when you round the corner, you are moved to a different lane. The lanes shift with each turn, until, finally, they all merge.

You often look at acts of violence from only one perspective. Wonderful things can sometimes come out of these situations. Look at the events of September 11, 2001. Tremendous amounts of Love, cooperation, trust, and unity were born from the ashes of negativity. The people of New York City now do not even panic "when the lights go out." When you look at the grand scheme of things, there is no wrong road, only wrong perceptions.

## The Roadblock of Chaos

The terrorist attack of 9/11 brought everyone in the United States face-to-face with chaos. The unthinkable had happened in your very own country. Suddenly, confusion, clamor, pandemonium, and chaos reigned supreme. Were you no longer safe even at work in an office? Anywhere? What could you do? Where could you go to be safe?

There is a battle in your country and in the world between "control" and "chaos." Because chaos is unpredictable and cannot be trusted, people feel the need to push it as far out of their existence as possible. Governments jump at the first sign of chaos and use it as an excuse to impose stricter laws and regulations on everybody, even though 99.8 percent of the population did not create the chaos. People are led to believe they must submit to these rules and regulations, or chaos will reign. Yet chaos will heal much faster if people do not have resistance to it. This resistance creates a solid wall against the energy of chaos that would like to heal.

Chaos encompasses a form of powerful energy that would like to heal…that needs to heal…in order to bring the Creator's Love onto the Earth. It is seeking its right place, and if allowed to move and gain even a small degree of acceptance, chaos would cease, believe it or not. The followers of the dark cousins are involved in keeping up the roadblock against chaos because they know how powerful chaos can be to pull Love onto the Earth. These dark followers even create situations of chaos at times in order to gain more control over people. These dark cousins hold great walls of resistance against chaos because of a terror they hold in their hearts of losing control over you.

## The Movement for Acceptance

Yet regardless of their view of chaos, there is a movement afoot by ordinary people who have begun to embrace chaos. Perhaps the '60s children who "dropped out" of mainstream society to "go with the flow" started it. After the 9/11 terrorist attack these many years later, there was a spontaneous initial response across the country that took the form of signs everywhere, reading "God Bless America" rather than "kill the terrorists."

God will bless America because of that initial response. When people allow themselves to accept and feel the negative emotions that chaos seems to create, these emotions begin to move. They begin to express themselves for what they really are underneath—love! Yes, what a surprise. Chaos conceals a thwarted Love that needs to be embraced, not stomped upon. In fact, a great deal of what you view as chaos is actually an illusion coming from your own perceptions and your fear of reality. You are afraid that chaos would result if you left this illusion. America and most Western nations have been living in an illusion that things are fine on Earth and that there is no need to change.

*If You Drive Off The Road, Can You Get Back On?*

## Things Are Not What They Seem

We say, "Wake up, Children of Earth!" Things are not what they seem. You are destroying your environment. You are raising your children to think only of themselves. Your military and industrial establishments are gobbling up precious resources that could benefit all of mankind with homes for the homeless, food for the hungry, opportunities for those in poverty, and cures for those with incurable diseases. Your chemicals are poisoning your food sources and your water. Even your weather seems out of control. But most important of all, you continue to ignore your connection with your Creator and Mother Earth. You keep yourselves disconnected from the Source of Love. Wake up, Children of Earth! All is not well. You are living in an illusion.

If you leave this illusion, will you spin out of control on this grand road of yours? Not at all. The fabric of chaos can vanish like a puff of smoke when you allow Love. Accept chaos. Embrace it, and your lives will be transformed. Chaos represents the feminine, the right brain, creativity. For its power of Love to be expressed, it needs to feel compassion and acceptance, not resistance and roadblocks built of fear. You who find yourselves fearful of total chaos need to step back and observe. Before rushing out in a frenzy of terror, you need to take a deep breath and let yourselves stand silently while you regroup your own emotions.

What would happen if you were to help someone instead of taking up arms against the enemy? Would this change the way things might turn out? What would happen if you were to accept the confusion for a while rather than confront it in anger? Would this change your perceptions? Would it change the outcome?

## Whole Viewing

Indeed, it would. But people on Earth also need to understand the concept of "whole viewing." Whole viewing involves looking at everything that happens at the same time. If you were able to do that from your three-dimensional perspective, it would look completely chaotic. Most of your minds are not equipped for whole viewing. It is more than just an Earth distortion. It is the fact that most three-dimensional people do not have the capability.

Whole viewing is more connected to a higher dimensional level of viewing. In other words, if you are human, you are only seeing part of the picture on Earth. Whole viewing is the expanded version of whole feeling that we discussed earlier. You need to observe things from all perspectives.

You can always see more. By the acceptance that you are not seeing everything, you will begin to see more. Then by desiring and having intent, you will find yourself actually seeing and understanding more of what is happening around you. Those three words—*acceptance, desiring,* and *intent*—are important keys to whole viewing. Acceptance that you are not seeing everything is true humility. It means you do not assume that you know everything. Emotions are another key to whole viewing. Having strong feelings about something helps you to view it both internally and externally.

Some of you have heard author Janice tell the remarkable tale about the natives of Tierra del Fuego at the tip of South America when the first European explorers appeared so unexpectedly off their shore. When Ferdinand Magellan's ships anchored offshore, none of the natives could see them! Their minds were not open to the comprehension of anything as astounding as a sailing ship. So they saw nothing! Only the wise man, the shaman, could see the ships and describe them to his people, for he had developed the skill of whole viewing even with his eyes closed.

## *If You Drive Off The Road, Can You Get Back On?*

Do not laugh at the poor natives. How many of you have seen a so-called UFO? The same rules apply. Certain people see them, while others viewing the same area of the sky see nothing. The same happened with people in the movie *Field of Dreams*. Those practicing whole viewing saw the baseball players on the diamond in the cornfield. Those who did not saw only an empty ball field.

It is important for readers of this book to become aware of the concept of whole viewing. It will expand their thought processes and perhaps even expose some of the myths they have been holding onto.

## Crop Circles

Even mathematicians who followed the chaos theory research of Benoit Mandelbrot in the 1960s had their minds opened to whole viewing. By repeating simple mathematical formulas over and over, he found that beautiful images, now called fractal geometry, were produced. What started as chaos evolved into breathtaking images—some called Julia Sets, the Mandelbrot Set, and the Koch Curve Snowflake. Have you heard of them? They have all appeared as crop circles in England!

As Janice tells us, crop circle researcher Linda Moulton Howe wonders, "Could the crop circle formations be a warning, a mysterious language in mathematic code from an advanced intelligence that can see the future from a timeless place, understands the repetitive patterns of our space-time, and knows mankind is at a dangerous, self-destructive moment of the evolutionary spiral? Could human indifference to the life force that's being destroyed provoke a higher power to respond and intervene?"[1]

---

[1] Howe, L. M. (2000). *Mysterious Lights and Crop Circles*. New Orleans: Paper Chase Press.

We say the higher power is you. You need to wake up and see what is out there on your grand road to enlightenment. Mother Earth is calling you to take off your blinders and make the changes necessary to preserve yourselves and all humanity.

## Believe in Yourself: Change Directions

Think about what a detour is. It is a road that leads you through construction. What is construction? It is change. Detours are the points in your life that allow change. How can you affect these changes? With choice. We do not see choice in terms of good or bad, only choice. Some of you were born into or steered into negative life situations such as crime, prostitution, or drug abuse. You feel that you cannot escape this path, that you are stuck on this road. You feel that you are not worthy or deserving of Love. We say you are worthy.

Making the choice to change the direction of your life places you in the driver's seat on your road to enlightenment. Even if you detour back into the areas of construction, you are still worthy. Re-member, you are spiritual beings. Even though the flesh may be weak, you are honored for your role in the lesson. You hold many judgments against yourselves. You feel you are not worthy of Love, respect, or abundance. But you are. Believe in yourself, and the universe will open itself to you.

## Use Free Will to Choose Your Path

On the road to enlightenment, you have free will to choose your path. When you come to the construction areas of your life lessons, expect miracles. Allow the Creator in you to create a miracle. Drive into the sunset and allow yourself to see its beauty. See the beauty in yourself. See the beauty in the world around you. Bless the road you have been down. Honor the road that you are on now. Let your divine light enlighten your

*If You Drive Off The Road, Can You Get Back On?*

next choice. Above all else, know that you are always on the right road—the road that leads you Home.

## Keys to Whole Viewing

- *Acceptance (that you do not see everything)*
- *Desire (that you will see more)*
- *Intent (to see more, say it aloud)*
- *Emotion (strong feelings about seeing more)*
- *Belief (in yourself)*

*Speed Bumps on the Road to Enlightenment*

Blocks of fear
And walls of anger
Call all be healed
With tears of laughter;
And so it is released...

CHAPTER 6

# Cosmic Humor: Activate Your Funny Bone

A funny thing happened on the road to enlightenment. Your joy for life fell off the luggage rack. You carry a lot of baggage around with you. It is filled with stress, worry, doubt, and anxiety. You hold onto it tightly, strapping it down so it cannot get away. You try so hard to gain the best out of life that you forget to live life. You are so caught up in attaining the dream that you become a slave to the power engine of success. You start out with the dream of providing a wonderful life for yourself and your loved ones. But you become so obsessed with the goal that you don't enjoy the game. You lose yourself, your family, and your friends along the wayside. When you finally attain your so-called dream, there is no one left to share it with, and it becomes a hollow victory for you.

## Joy

You ask, "How do I get joy in my life?" We say you do not acquire joy; you allow joy to emerge. Joy is within the well of your soul. It is a part of you at birth. But as you evolve on the physical planet, you acquire layers of negativity that bury your joy inside you. Have you not noticed that when you laugh, it feels like something springing forth from inside you? The phrase "bubbles of laughter" is very appropriate. When you laugh, unseen bubbles of Love energy explode from inside you. Laughter is contagious. When someone near you is laughing, aren't you curious to know why? You feel drawn, not just by the sound of laughter, but by the energy it releases. You all crave joy. It was supposed to be a part of you, but the dark cousins fractured your funny bone.

Religion then was not as it is today. In fact, there was no religion per se. You all had your own inner connection to Spirit. Your church was nature. Your religious service was simply joy: joy of life, joy of the Earth. Re-member, we told you in Chapter 1 that the dark cousins assumed god-like status. They masqueraded as benevolent gods and established religion. Religion was the first form of government. It was all about control.

## Misrepresentation of Religion

Prior to the arrival of the dark cousins, there was no need for government. You lived in harmony. The early religions advocated fear and sacrifice to appease the gods. So it was for millennia. This misrepresentation of religion was a part of you for so long that it became a standard in the formation of all religions. Your religious texts are full of stories of vengeful gods, sacrifice, and guilt.

## Let Laughter Rise Up

But you have come a long way. Fear is no longer a factor in many religions. Love and joy are again taking their rightful place. The old walls of religious control are crumbling, and they are being replaced by a sense of community. This community is filled with light beings who are you. To get to the light inside you, all you need to do is to laugh. Let laughter rise up through the layers of negativity. As it rises, it creates holes and tunnels, which allow your inner light to shine.

Look for the humor around you, especially in nature. Have you ever watched baby animals at play—puppies, kittens, monkeys, deer? No matter where you are, there are examples of boundless joy in nature. Look also at small children. Joy is a state of being you were all born with. You need to re-member that joy is another one of your birthrights. You need to activate your funny bone.

Julie says, "Even Creator has a sense of humor. Look at a picture of a duck-billed platypus or a baboon's bottom. These are funny things. Many things in life are absurd. They invite you to laugh. Look for the absurdity around you, and enjoy."

## Look for the Absurdities in Life

We agree—look for the absurdities in your own life. You write many absurd situations into your life plan. Think about the expression "lighten up." It is a direct reference to allowing the light, the joy, to rise up inside you. You have become too serious. Your higher selves literally trip you up on occasion.

Have you ever been walking down a sidewalk and tripped over nothing? Your first instinctive response is to look around to see if anyone saw you do it. You feel embarrassed. Next time this happens, look around to see what Spirit wants you to notice. Look within yourself to see what you are being so serious about. These "trips" usually happen when you are miles away, lost in thought, worrying or obsessing over something. We say lighten up. Allow humor and beauty into your life. They will enable joy to arise within you no matter how gloomy you are.

## The Money Trap

Money has been used to trap your emotional essence, your spiritual essence. These lost essences need to come back to you. The money trap is not entirely of your own making. The followers of the dark cousins are intricately involved in your money situation. They feed on your vulnerability and frustration.

Most spiritual people feel they should not accumulate money, nor even want it. Yet in this money-dominated society, it seems to be a necessary evil in order to live. Yet even people with a great deal of money are caught in the trap. Millionaires often lead desperate lives because they lack Love. You need to take your judgments off people who have money. A poor family with Love that has compassion for the rich man who has no Love is better off in the long run. Then there are the millions of Third World people who live in hopeless poverty, while your Western world has abundance.

First, you need to see that all of this suffering over money, or the lack of it, is larger than you are. It is a global situation. Not only is it personal with everyone, it is killing people's hearts. It is a dark force that has made people on Earth vulnerable.

## Stay in Your Heart

There is an answer to the situation, but it lies within you—in your heart. It is imperative that you stay in your heart while seeking this resolution. Otherwise, you will be caught in your left brain where negative feelings about money originate.

Everything in your society set up by the dark cousins is designed to give the brain power. But it is in the heart that real changes can be made. The biggest challenge of humanity is to stay in the heart, not the brain.

You are not able to see the whole picture right now, but the money trap is the core issue of struggle and strife on the planet. Because you cannot contain all the energy in this dense "ball of yarn," we suggest that you accept the fact that it is inconceivable to your brain and that only your heart can lead you through it. You are not even meant to see all that is involved in this trap, for there are setups within the ball of yarn to prevent its unraveling. Ask for Love to go before you as you try to extricate yourself from this trap.

## Do Enjoyable Things

To begin with, you should continue life by doing things you love to do, that make you feel good, that give you pleasure—even if you don't have money and even if it is for brief periods. Have fun with one another. Laugh. Enjoy yourselves. Take your mind off your money worries. That is where you are vulnerable.

You have something to learn about your vulnerability. Strange as it may seem, you have to nurture it. You have to tell it that things are going to get better. Help is coming. Worrying about money will only add to your desperation, suffering, and tension. You, too, will be caught up in this knotted ball of yarn. When you find yourself worrying about money and how you will have enough to pay all your bills, stop. That is your left brain talking. Take a deep breath and try to get down into your heart. Try to feel Love. Ask the Creator to be with you. Say aloud and with passion, "God be with me in my money worries!" Then think of things that give you pleasure and make you laugh.

## Look at the Beauty of Nature

What can you do to let Love flow through your being? Pretend you are an artist such as Monet or Van Gogh. Look at the beauty of nature with new eyes: the colored leaves of autumn, a dandelion in the crack of the sidewalk, a sunrise, a sunset, a tree lifting its branches skyward, clouds in all their myriad shapes. Can you re-member what you thought about clouds as a child? How you found dragons and antelopes floating across the sky? Bring into your heart the happiness of childhood memories, when everything was fresh, new, and lovely.

## Observe Your Vulnerability

Now you must try to feel your vulnerability again—but as an outside observer. What does it feel like? What does it look like? Think of words to describe it: "dense," "rough around the edges," "like a villain in a black cloak from an old-time melodrama tiptoeing around inside my head," "like a pair of open handcuffs ready to snap shut."

Can you visualize that? Say these words aloud with vigor! Treat your vulnerability as a real old-fashioned villain, a robber. Tell him what you think of him in no uncertain terms. You are acting out a drama.

## Pretend to Be Robbers

Get your partner and your children involved. Tell them they should all pretend to be old-fashioned robbers with bulging packs on their backs, tiptoeing around in their brains looking for money to steal. Have everyone get up and move around. Make it fun and funny. How will they get rid of these robbers? Make them fall in a mud puddle? Put them in a washing machine and turn on the "heavy" cycle? No shooting or violence is allowed—only solutions that will make you all end up laughing. And how do the robbers end up? Flat on their backs with the bulging packs bursting open, erupting money over everything!

Every time money worries get the best of you, try enacting another drama such as this. But be sure you end up laughing. For as the great comic-philosopher Mark Twain has told you, "Against the assault of laughter nothing can stand."

We asked Janice for the whole quote from Twain's book The Mysterious Stranger (1916). He has Satan saying, "Your race, in its poverty, has unquestionably one really effective weapon—laughter. Power, money, persuasion, supplication, persecution—these can lift a colossal humbug—push it a little—weaken it a little, century by century; but only laughter can blow it to rags and atoms at a blast. Against the assault of laughter nothing can stand."

## Self-Fulfilling Prophecy

Believing that your money situation will get better helps to make it better. It is a self-fulfilling prophecy that can help to overcome the problem. But worrying about it keeps your frustrations locked in your brain and prevents your heart from interacting with the Source of Love. Laughter truly unlocks the heart. Even Twain's Tom Sawyer knew what a healer it was: "Such a laugh was money in a man's pocket, because it cut down on the doctor's bills like everything." Now, you try it.

## Keys to Extricating Yourself from the Money Trap

- *Do not worry about money.*
- *Try to get down into your heart and feel Love.*
- *Ask God to be with you. (Say with passion: "God, help me get out of this money trap!")*
- *Look at the beauty of nature with new eyes.*
- *Enact or visualize a drama of an old-fashioned robber with a bulging money sack that bursts open in a hilarious ending.*
- *Believe sincerely that your money situation will get better.*
- *Laugh! Laugh! Laugh!*

## Music

We want you to cry tears of laughter. Laugh until your sides hurt. The pain is a release of pent-up emotions. Laugh until you cry. Tears not only release negative emotions; they wash toxins from your system. Sing a silly song. Music both sung and listened to is a powerful tool of release. Music is emotion that reflects and imitates your vibration. Re-member, your inner being is composed of light and vibration. Your very soul responds to vibrations both good and bad.

Music has wonderful healing properties. It can be used to retool your vibrations when they get out of sync. Like the wobble of the Earth on its axis, your vibrations are affected by outside stimuli. You become out-of-ease, or diseased. Much illness could be cured if you re-membered how to retune yourself. Music that affects you in a positive way, that seems to resonate within you, is healing you on some level. The reverse is also true. Music can make you feel disharmony and negative feelings.

The followers of the dark cousins are still plying their trade. Negative music has been targeted at young, impressionable minds. Many of you parents are aware of this and are already taking steps to stop it.

## Music of the Masters

On the positive side, many ascended masters have come to Earth as great composers—Beethoven, Bach, and Mozart, to name a few. Much of the music they composed was to promote healing and raise the vibrations of their time. Mankind was evolving quickly and needed to raise its vibrations in order to receive more of the Love vibration. People needed to raise their frequencies before stepping into the industrial and technological centuries. Technological advancement without spiritual involvement can be a deadly game. Atlantis is a testament to this.

Janice says Mark Twain had something to say about music in the late nineteenth century as well. He had great reservations about Wagner's music. He disliked it. He wrote about attending the Wagner opera *Lohengrin* in his book *A Tramp Abroad* (1879): "The banging and slamming and booming and crashing were something beyond belief. The racking and pitiless pain of it remains stored up in my memory alongside the memory of the time I had my teeth fixed… When one was hoping the singers might come to an understanding and modify their noise, a great chorus composed entirely of maniacs would suddenly break forth, and then during two minutes, and sometimes three, I lived over again all that I had suffered the time the orphan asylum burned down."

Twain did admit to liking parts of it: "We only had one brief little season of heaven and heaven's sweet ecstasy and peace during all this long and diligent and acrimonious reproduction of the other place. This was when a gorgeous procession of people marched around and sang the Wedding

Chorus. While my seared soul was steeped in the healing balm of those gracious sounds, it seemed to me that I could almost re-suffer the torments which had gone before, in order to be so healed."

The vibrations of Wagner's music were definitely Germanic—very strong and very military-like. When we think of the two world wars that followed in the twentieth century and learn that Hitler was a fan of Wagner, we are led to wonder if the dark cousins did not plant Wagner on Earth to sway humans towards exhibiting military strength and fighting.

## Art

Appreciating the beauty of art is another way of allowing joy to rise within you. Many artists have been ascended masters who used art to provoke emotions: Michelangelo, who showed mankind the beauty of the human form in his sculptures; da Vinci, who blended glorious art and amazing technology with his inventions; Monet, Degas, and Van Gogh, who discovered new ways of incorporating light into their paintings; and even Picasso, who helped mankind make a dimensional leap with the scattered vibrations of his twentieth century art. All played their roles.

## The Beauty of Nature

The release of emotions helps clear the body to receive more light. Mother Nature is the grandest of artists. Many try to imitate her but fail in comparison. You need to use all your senses to appreciate nature. See the beauty and humor she displays to you. Hear her music: the sighing of wind through trees, the babbling of a brook, and the first bird at dawn. Feel her complexity: all the different textures of Earth, such as stones, sand, leaves, tree bark, and crystals. Smell her perfumes: the scent of flowers, the fresh sea breeze, the smell of damp

## Cosmic Humor: Activate Your Funny Bone

earth in the forest. And taste her essences: succulent fruits, wholesome grains, crunchy nuts, savory herbs, pure water. The bounties of nature can enable joy to rise within you. But most of all, you must *laugh, laugh, laugh!*

## Spontaneity

How many of you have ever acted in a spontaneous manner? You know—clicked your heels as you walked down the street or sang a little song as you waited on a corner for the bus? Or did a little dance on your front porch before starting out in the morning? Most people have lost their spontaneity along with their sense of humor. You all take yourselves and your lives too seriously. Loosen up. Lighten up. Let your feelings out. Let that hidden joy bubble up.

Next time you walk down the street, what about doing a little skipping or playing a bit of hopscotch? Are you afraid people will laugh at you? Let them! Join in with them, and invite them to join in with you. Or face them and take a bow. That should get them! A spontaneous reaction such as this breaks up something dense inside that needs to get out.

How many of you have seen "the wave" done by spectators at sporting events? Have you ever participated? Then you know how you felt afterwards—lighter, happier, often laughing with everyone. "The wave" was a spontaneous action originally started by a group of people at a football game. Now everyone does it because he or she enjoys it. But it is still spontaneous.

You will find unexpected delights in spontaneous actions such as this because it feels so good. When you participate with others, it feels even better because you are tuned into the feelings of everyone. Something good is happening inside you as well. Toxins are being released, and you are being brought into sync with the Source of Love.

*Speed Bumps on the Road to Enlightenment*

Spontaneity is a lot like joy. If you search for it, you will not find it. You just have to let it happen.

## Five Simple Rules to Break

### 1. *Adults must be serious.*

*We say, "Re-member, you are supposed to be Children of the Earth, and children are supposed to be playful. That bottle of bubbles is not just for your children or grandchildren. Blow them for yourself or for your pets. Dogs and cats love to chase bubbles. Fly a kite. Make a snow angel. Don't put the crayons away. Color a smile on your face.*

### 2. *Dessert is for after dinner.*

*Indulge yourself occasionally. Feed the child within. Let that piece of pie become his meal once in a while.*

### 3. *The good china is only for special occasions.*

*Any day can be a special occasion. If the beautiful things you own bring you joy, use them. Don't lock them away for "someday." Someday may never come. Allow beauty to become a part of your everyday life.*

### 4. *Work first, play later.*

*Those two hours away from work to see your child at play will not break you. The dishes can wait. Read that story. Take that walk. Do not separate work and play times. Incorporate fun into your workday. We know many of you have very serious jobs. But you need to let your child-self breathe. Make a funny face in the mirror when you go to the washroom. Allow fantasy and mystery. Wear boxer shorts with balloons on them under your dark suit. Become the office happy bandit. Leave little notes of encouragement, silly pictures, or pieces of candy around. Then join in the mystery of trying to figure out who did it.*

5. ***Children should be seen and not heard.***
*Listen to children. Talk to children. Encourage imagination. Today's children have forgotten how to imagine. Video and television do it for them. Have imaginary tea parties. Howl like coyotes and bark like dogs. Pretend. Pretend. Pretend. Unlock their minds to the possibilities of all things and you will open yourself to possibilities and joy.*

## Games of the Heart for Grownups

Janice tells us that she has invented a whole series of games designed for adults to play in order to open their hearts to laughter and Love. Here is one of them.

### *Heart Charades*

"Charades was a favorite parlor game of the Clemens clan in their big Hartford living room. Mark Twain, one of the greatest wordsmiths of all time, was in his glory thinking up impossibly long words and acting out the syllables himself for his children, wife, and friends to guess. His girls, on the other hand, actually dressed up in costumes to dramatize their own words."

"Heart Charades doesn't ask you to make it such a big production. Just think up some heart words with the power to make you feel emotion. If you can visualize the words, then you can feel the emotion behind them."

"First, *turn off the television!* You and a partner can then choose a secret heart word and act it out in pantomime, syllable by syllable. Use your hands to speak for you, stretching them apart to show your audience how long or short the word

## Speed Bumps on the Road to Enlightenment

is, holding up fingers to show how many syllables it has, and which syllable you are pantomiming. No talking. You can nod your head "yes" or shake it "no" each time someone asks a question or shouts out a guess. If you're playing with children in the group, make some of the words one-syllable ones like "kiss" and "hug."

"What are some heart words? They can be any words that make you feel an emotion. You may want to choose a category of heart words ahead of time, such as "funny" or "love" or "happy," with words such as these:

| **Funny** | **Love** | **Happy** |
|---|---|---|
| Droll | Hug | Bright |
| Silly | Kiss | Glad |
| Witty | Love | Cheerful |
| Wacky | Adore | Joyful |
| Laughable | Boyfriend | Cherry |
| Ludicous | Girlfriend | Delighted |
| Comical | Darling | Thrilled |
| Farcical | Embrace | Jolly |
| Amusing | Romance | Jovial |
| Hilarious | Sweetheart | Merry |
| Humorous | Heartfelt | Gleeful |
| Hysterical | Heartthrob | Jubilant |
| Ridiculous | Heartstring | Elated |
| Madcap | Affection | Ecstatic |
| A hoot | Romantic | Overjoyed |

"Make it fun and funny. How would you dramatize "adore," for instance? Hold up two fingers for two syllables.

## Cosmic Humor: Activate Your Funny Bone

Point to your second finger, meaning second syllable. Then pantomime opening a door. If no one guesses right, make it funnier by trying to open a door that is stuck. Whoever gets it right can choose a partner and a new secret heart word."

### Dear-to-the-Heart Charades

A final game you might consider is 'Dear-to-the-Heart Charades.'" This game focuses on plants and animals that are dear to your heart. The speaker tells the onlookers to close their eyes for about twenty seconds and visualize a plant or animal that is especially dear to their hearts, perhaps a favorite pet or tree or flower. Whatever comes into your visual imagery is fine. Since my special interest is birds, I was not surprised to have a great blue heron stalk across my imagination.

Then, one at a time, the players stand up and dramatize their vision. I had fun stalking jerkily in front of the group with my clasped-together hands at my face, pointing forward like the stiletto beak of a large heron and darting down to stab a fish. Everyone guessed it easily, and one person even saw the same image. If players have allowed images to come to them, they tend to be quite powerful visualizations with emotions attached. Tell the players to call up these images anytime they need to feel something dear to their hearts.

What if they visualize people? We tend to hold so many judgments and comparisons about the people in our lives that these images may be best kept private and not done in a group. Animals are easier to dramatize in funny ways, and you don't want to make fun of people.

> Although this ability to make visual imagery seems to come from the brain, it is the head's connection to the heart that allows the energy to flow, which others on the same wavelength are sometimes able to pick up. Are you? Try playing Dear-to-the-Heart Charades with good companions and see what happens. And laugh, laugh, laugh!

*Cosmic Humor: Activate Your Funny Bone*

## Speed Bumps on the Road to Enlightenment

Feed me knowledge,
More, more, more,
Yoga, meditation,
And books galore;
And so it is gathered...

CHAPTER 7

# Becoming A Metaphysical Junkie: Feed Me More Knowledge

Your quest for knowledge is as natural to you as breathing. Knowledge is nourishment to the soul, just as food is to the physical body. Re-member from Chapter 1 that we told you the common theme of Creation is to gather knowledge. As the veil starts to thin and you see glimpses of your true self, you thirst for more. The more you know, the greater your thirst. As you gain knowledge, you begin to think less like a human and more like the spiritual beings that you are. The fact that you are reading this book is a testament to your quest for knowledge.

## New Age Concepts

The road to enlightenment is filled with billboards showing attractions and services at the various exits. The signs differ depending at which point of the road you are. You are all on your own unique journey, and the knowledge you gather is suitable for you at that particular point. Many of you started on your journey with involvement in a particular religion. As involved as you were, you felt something lacking, that there was more to the big picture. First, you explored other religions that utilized different techniques, such as meditation or faith healing. This then led you to try an alternative healing for an ailment. You said, "Hey, this really works!" You discovered that these so-called New Age ways of thinking and healing are actually ancient re-membrances.

The New Age concepts resonated within you. Your inner self said, "I know this, and I want to know more!" You find yourself reading two or three books at a time. Your hunger is great. For long periods, you keep this hunger to yourself. Even though you believe how the universe is meant to be, you are still influenced by the male, aggressive, fear-controlling energy. You fear ridicule. Depending on the community you live in, you may even fear open hostility.

## Times Are Changing

But times are truly changing. Mass media, for all its so-called negativity, has allowed people from all walks of life to gain exposure to all kinds of concepts. Ignorance has ever been the control mechanism for the dark cousins. But they are losing ground. Ignorance breeds fear, which in turn breeds hostility. But ignorance is being taken out of the equation. Without the roots of ignorance, the branches of fear and hostility begin to wither and die. The human race is much more accepting of new concepts as, thanks to mass media, you are not striking out in fear of the unknown.

As you overcome your fears and begin to talk to people, you realize how many people of like mind are in your community. Alternative thinking is fast becoming the norm, not the exception. The greatest source for gaining knowledge is to re-member.

## RE-MEMBER

    **R**...recall

    **E**...earlier

    **M**...memories

    **E**...expect

    **M**...miracles

    **B**...be

    **E**...enthusiastic

    **R**...rejoice

## Trust Yourself

We have noticed that many of you are looking outside of yourselves for enlightenment. You think that if you practice some religion or master some technique, the knowledge of the universe will descend upon you. There are many useful tools, but re-member, you are the lockbox that they open. Do not look to others to provide the answers for you. Everyone is on his own unique journey, and someone else's truth may not be yours.

You need to trust yourself. Trust and believe in yourself. Re-member, a Spark of Creator is within you. Yes, you contain within yourselves the knowledge of All That Is. But you have been misled into not trusting yourselves, not thinking for yourselves. For millennia, the dark cousins have enslaved your will. You have been programmed how to think and feel. You have become so used to control that you incorporate control into your own lives and pass it on to your children.

How many of you have said to a child, "Stop crying," "That's not funny," "Isn't that sad?" You impose your concepts of emotion on them instead of allowing them to express how they really feel. You all express counterfeit emotions. You need to learn how to express genuine feelings. You need to trust yourselves.

## Recall Earlier Memories

You have heard of tantric sex where couples touch and explore each other's body to gain true ecstasy between them. We want you to practice "tantric feelings" using the first key phrase in RE-MEMBER: *recall earlier memories*. This practice cannot be done all at once, for you will be discovering varied emotions.

Starting at your forehead, gently run your fingertips over it. How does it feel? Does it tingle? Make you itch? Now, what is the emotion behind the sensation? Nervousness? Embarrassment? Fear? Look beyond the emotion. Is it attached to an event earlier in your life? Is there a scar? How did you acquire it? Did you express your true emotions at the time, or were you told, "That doesn't hurt. Stop crying. It was an accident; there's no reason to get mad." Recall, re-member, and release the trapped emotions.

Work your way down your body: face, neck, arms, torso, genitals, legs, and feet. Take your time over areas where traumas (scars) have occurred. Reach into your memories to see if there are trapped emotions there. Don't just look for the negative emotions. Re-experience the positive ones also. The burdens of life often bury the good memories. When you touch your lip, re-member that first kiss. When you caress your shoulders and arms, re-member being hugged as a child or being held in the arms of a loved one. Re-member that part of you that looked at the world with awe and wonder. Relive that feeling of just being happy for no particular reason.

## Counterfeit Emotions

When you release the trapped memories and emotions, you will be able to fill the spaces with Love energy. As you cleanse the counterfeit emotions and get to the essence of the true you, many things will come into perspective. The counterfeit emotions have caused you not to trust your feelings. From there, the mistrust spread. You began to mistrust what you saw and what you heard.

Spirit is all around you, and it has made itself known to you all your life. When the veil has thinned, and you have seen glimpses of other worlds, you will say, "I didn't see that. I didn't hear that. It was a figment of my imagination." We say, "Claim your trust again. Relive your memories and glean from them the keys of knowledge."

### Did That Really Happen?

Julie had a did-that-really-happen event in her life. She would like to share it with you.

"In May of 2001, just prior to our marriage, John moved to New Hampshire with me. I had borrowed my brother's huge Suburban to fetch him and all his stuff. We were crossing a narrow bridge at the same time as a tractor pulling an oversized piece of farm equipment. The equipment was swaying back and forth, and we had to move to the extreme right to avoid having our side-view mirror taken off. In doing so, the passenger-side tires slipped off the pavement. Not only were we not stuck, but also I actually saw the guardrail bend outward so it wouldn't scratch the truck. My first instinct was to think, 'No way, that couldn't have happened.' But it did."

*Speed Bumps on the Road to Enlightenment*

This incident jogs Janice's mind to re-member a did-that-really-happen event in her own life. Julie re-members this one, too.

> We had both driven down to Santa Fe from our home in Taos, New Mexico, to go shopping in the Villa Linda Mall. After dinner, and just as it was becoming dark, we started back with me (Janice) at the wheel. I had to make a left turn into the very wide Rodeo Drive, so I waited until the traffic in the three left lanes had stopped a block down at a traffic light. Then I made my turn and found myself behind another left-turner in what I thought was a turning lane. But it wasn't.
>
> Suddenly, Julie was shouting, "Look out, Jan, he's coming right at you!" The traffic light must have changed, and three lanes of cars were speeding towards us. There was one car in the innermost lane that was fast approaching us head-on. I could not do anything. The car in front still had not moved. So there I sat, waiting for the crash. Julie re-members the glare of his headlights almost upon us, when suddenly he was gone. He didn't hit us or go around us, but there he was going down the road behind us, just as if we hadn't been there. Whoa!

## Expect Miracles

This leads us to the second key phrase in RE-MEMBER: *expect miracles.* Your lives are full of them. Miracles are cosmic magic. You don't need to have intervention by God, saints, or angels. You just need to believe in yourself. Believe in the fact that all things are possible. When you start to really re-member your life, look for your miracles. You created them.

Sometimes, your higher selves ask for angelic intervention. Many books have been written about how angels appeared and saved someone during a fearful or dangerous moment. Fear of dying, fear of illness, and fear of injury often trigger miracles. But fear is the *counterfeit emotion* here. Love is what actually triggers miracles. You create miracles to help those you love. You create miracles to help yourself. Yes, you are worthy of miracles. Do not think miracles are only huge and outstanding events. It is often the tiny miracles, barely noticed, that are the most significant in your life.

How many times in your life have you said, "I passed that test; it was a miracle." Or, "That stone just missed me by a fraction of an inch. It was a miracle." Or, "My cat fell out of a second-story window and didn't get hurt. It must have been a miracle." Guess what? It *was* a miracle. They were all miracles. Even though you said the words, you did not trust it to be so. You did not believe that a miracle could have happened to a plain, simple nobody.

You have been conditioned for so long into seeing greatness only in figures of power and authority that you do not see yourselves as the beautiful, complex beings that you are. We want to give you a fresh look at being a nobody. No-body. Without a body, what are you? Spirit! Stop thinking like a human and more like the no-body that you are. We are starting a "wave" here on our side of the veil for no-bodies. Join the wave, and see how many miracles you notice.

*Speed Bumps on the Road to Enlightenment*

## Dreams

Dreams are the mass transit system on the road to enlightenment. They are the subways through your subconscious and the Orient Express to Home. Many of you think that you do not dream. This is not so. As we told you previously, the dream state is where you keep in contact with your higher selves, your soul group, and your extraterrestrial family. It is where you receive healing and nourishment for your soul and are able to access knowledge. For those of you who can re-member your dreams, you need to keep track of them.

Because of the veil of forgetfulness, you do not get the full message all in one dream. But as you catalogue them, you will see a pattern emerge that will allow you to access the hidden knowledge. If you cannot re-member your dreams, you need to state your intent to do so. You need to say, "I give myself the gift of re-membering my dreams. I accept this gift with an open heart. There are no ribbons of fear or bows of anxiety. This gift is wrapped in pure Love."

As you say this intent, visualize a box wrapped in shiny, beautiful paper. As the paper falls away and you lift off the lid, you become enveloped in a warm, glowing light and the most wonderful aroma you have ever smelled. You feel nothing but endless Love.

Say this as often as you need to. If you have been denying your dreams for years, it may take a little while to break through that roadblock you have erected. Even if you do have good dream recall, this intent and visualization will help you re-member even more.

Dreams also help you to process your daily life. Let's take a closer look at the word dreams.

*Becoming A Metaphysical Junkie*

**D**...digest
**R**...reorganize
**E**...eliminate
**A**...assimilate
**M**...manage
**S**....store

Here is how they work. First, your subconscious *digests*. It takes in all the events of the day. Then it *reorganizes* them all. Situations in your life come in a haphazard jumble. There is no set time of day when only good things come at you or bad things. Life just happens. After your subconscious reorganizes everything into groups, it *eliminates* what is not necessary, such as routine things you have already processed. Next, your subconscious *assimilates* what is left. It gathers in the energy and knowledge that the lesson provided.

After assimilating the knowledge, your subconscious *manages* the information. Like an office manager, it places the knowledge gained in its proper place, where it is then *stored* in the brain, the heart, and the cells. Dreams are the modem for life lessons.

## Dreams Work Out Conflicts

The dream state is also a neutral ground where you can work out conflict with friends, coworkers, and family. In dreams, you can often vent emotions that you are incapable of venting otherwise. After an emotionally charged dream, you will be able to deal with that person in a much calmer way.

## Dreams Are Like Channeling

Dreams are also a form of channeling. You are receiving information in an unconscious state. People who go into a hypnotic trance or altered state to channel are actually entering into the dream state. In these altered states, you plug into your higher self. Your higher self exists in the now, where the knowledge of All That Is originates.

## Dream Dictionaries Are Useful

Dream dictionaries can be useful tools for interpreting dream symbols dealing with daily conflicts. Much symbolism is common to all. But dreams of a prophetic nature need to be viewed in their entirety. You need to write them down over a period to be able to see the whole picture. Re-member, dreams are the greatest source for gaining knowledge. They are a gift from you to yourself. Janice, who from time to time has kept lengthy dream journals and spent time interpreting them, has a few hints about what to look for.

A person's dream can only be interpreted by the person, but here are a few useful hints that are common to many dreams::

- People in your dreams whom you know well often represent themselves, but they can also symbolize aspects of you.

- People in your dreams whom you recognize but have not seen in a while usually represent not themselves but an aspect of you.

- A car or vehicle often represents you and your life. If it is speeding, it means you are going too fast; going uphill is positive; going downhill is negative; stalling out means that is what you are doing.

- A house can also symbolize you, with its rooms being aspects of you. Going upstairs is positive. Going downstairs is negative. An attic is often your spiritual self, a kitchen, your health. (I once dreamed that the chimney was on fire, and I woke up with a sore throat!)
- Be aware of incongruities. They are important. Also, look for puns, plays on words, and other kinds of humor. The subconscious can be funny.

If you don't re-member your dreams, don't worry; they are still working for you through your subconscious self. But it is more fun (and enlightening) to re-member them consciously and follow their advice. Many of your dreams may turn out to be precognitive; that is, showing you something that is going to happen in the future—maybe the next day, the next week, or in a year. So if you do record your dreams, go back over them every week or month to see if their happenings came true. If you don't re-member or record your dreams, think what you are missing—a huge chunk of your life!

## Be Enthusiastic

The third key phrase in RE-MEMBER is be *enthusiastic*. Be enthusiastic on your journey to enlightenment. Let there be joy in your quest for knowledge. Many of you become downhearted because you cannot master a technique. You often have feelings of jealousy toward someone who is able to do something you cannot do. You hunger so much to be able to do channeling, healing, or some other metaphysical gift that you unintentionally bury it with these negative emotions. You need to stay enthusiastic and look at the gift as something to look forward to, not something that you have missed.

You must re-member that there are degrees and dimensions to all things. You may already be that healer. It may not present itself in some grand and glorious way, but it is there nonetheless. Maybe you have a knack for saying just the right thing to someone that calms or makes him or her happier. That is a healing. Your words calm or diffuse a situation. You affected a change for the better. A talent such as this is no less important than someone who cures a disease. In fact, it is more important, because you are helping to prevent disease.

Layers of negativity are often the root of disease. When you cut the root, disease cannot take hold. Look within and claim your special talent. Trust in yourself. Believe in yourself. Recognize the miracles that you helped to create. Look forward to the new things you will learn, but be enthusiastic about the talents you already have.

## Rejoice

The final key phrase in RE-MEMBER is simply one word: *rejoice*. Be happy and proud of who you already are—wonderful, spiritual beings!

*Becoming A Metaphysical Junkie*

## Speed Bumps on the Road to Enlightenment

Instant total
Gratification;
"I want it now!"
Is the cry of nations;
And so, it is demanded....

CHAPTER 8

# Are We There Yet?

We have told you many times throughout this book that you are the children of the universe, and like children, you are impatient. You want things to happen *now*. In fact, you want things to happen yesterday. We know you are tired of hearing "all good things come to those who wait." Have you never wondered why they said "good things?" When you wait for something, it gives you time to grow and learn. When you receive something after a long struggle or wait, you appreciate it even more. When something is hard won, you honor and respect it. If you acquire something too easily, and you are not fully prepared, that good thing often becomes a bad thing.

## Instant Gratification: A Disease

Look around you. How much chaos do you see every day? Instant, total gratification has become a disease among mankind. There are many facets to this disease: debt, bankruptcy, divorce, crime, poverty, drug abuse, broken families...the list goes on. They do not stand alone. They feed off one another in a chaotic chain reaction. Many of you have firsthand knowledge of how this chain drags you down. And the followers of the dark cousins are there encouraging you along.

First, you get that great job with lots of overtime. Then you find the perfect house, a little bit beyond your range. But, hey, they have what they call "creative financing." And, of course, you just have to have that new car every two years. You upgrade from videos to DVDs because everyone else does. That recreational vehicle is a must, as is that yearly cruise and that skiing trip. That jacket in the window of the department store—now, you really cannot live without that. Everyone in the family has to have his or her own TV and cell phone.

## What Happens to Your Children?

About now, you are working seventy hours a week instead of forty or fifty. You begin feeling guilty about not seeing your kids, so you buy them more stuff and give them more money. But they don't have to do anything for it. No chores. No community service time. They follow your example. They want. They acquire. But they do not earn. Even though you are over-extended, at least you are actively working for things you want.

You are doing your children great harm by not setting limits. They need to work. They need to earn the right to receive things. When things come too easily or freely to them, they do not respect them. They do not learn to care for or conserve things. Their attitude is, "If it breaks or I lose it, my parents will get another for me." As you consistently give in to their demands, they lose respect for you. They lose respect for themselves. They have nothing to give them a sense of pride or accomplishment.

Loss of respect coupled with instant gratification breeds disaster. Boredom sets in. They have everything there is and nothing to look forward to. But, hey, that guy over there says he can show them a good time. Just one drink, one pill, one puff, and then "poof." Before you know it, you don't recognize that sullen individual who used to be your happy child.

You know that something is wrong, but right now, your life is in crisis. That overtime is no longer there. Your seventy-five-hour budget doesn't fit into your forty-hour life. You go cold turkey on all your personal spending. Your teenagers are not only sullen but also angry because you have cut down the money tree. They look for new avenues to support their habits—such as crime and prostitution.

## A Crash to Reality

Before you know it, one of your vehicles is repossessed. You file for bankruptcy. Stress is eating away at you. Tempers are short. Your blood pressure is high. And you have acid reflux. You start playing the blame game. With so much pressure, you cannot gather your wits to heal the wounds. So, you end up in divorce court. Now you have sullen, angry, and resentful teenagers with a dose of fear mixed in for good measure. The one positive factor in all this mess is that in the court-imposed family counseling, your teen's addictions have come to light.

You sell the house you could not afford in the first place. And the custody battles begin. At about this time, one of two things happens: your personal life has interfered at work once too often and you are fired, or your company downsizes and you are laid off. You manage to find a lower-paying job. You buy an older car and find a cheaper place to live. For a while, you mourn the life you had. Then you start to live again.

## A New Life
You are still scared about money, so you explore different pastimes rather than spending: free concerts in the park, long walks, and good books. Your children have found new outlets for their energy in community service, music, or sports. You are finally spending quality time with them. You are more of a family now than when you were under one roof.

You pause in mid-step one day. You think, "How can this be so? I'm happy! Why is that?" Because you have moved from the fast lane. You have entered a traffic pattern you can control, instead of it controlling you. You have time to breathe. You appreciate the little things in life, because you had to work to gain them.

## A New Awareness
We have told you before that there are dimensions and layers to all things. Your heart and brain have many layers. On the surface, you may think you are ready for it all. But in fact, all layers must be open and ready to receive. Many of you may think that the example we just told you about, "instant gratification," is extreme. It is not. In fact, it is an epidemic in your developed country.

Re-member, we told you earlier that you have to see the whole picture. This impatience and greed seems like a negative thing. It seems like you are feeding right into the hands of the dark cousins. But in fact, you are pulling the rug right out from underneath them. By setting you up for the fall, they are setting themselves up for the fall. Re-member, there is balance in all things. By orchestrating your poverty, they are creating their own. Bankruptcy is taking its toll on the financial community. They are panicking right now and don't want to let you know it.

As you are recovering after your crash to reality from your fantasy world, you begin using new conservation techniques. You spend less, using cash and little or no credit. When you come face-to-face with reality, you begin to see the reality in all things. You begin to practice conservation in all aspects of your life. You come to realize that less is more. You have opened awareness inside you. Your awareness opens the layers of your heart and brain. You are beginning to be able to see the whole picture. Even more than that, you are beginning to live the whole picture.

## The Instant Gratification Cycle

Everyone goes through the instant gratification cycle to some degree. At some point in your life, you all come up against the reality of want versus need. For many, it has to get to the extreme level as in the example we gave before the light of realization clicks on. Re-member, this is the planet of free will. And one of the aspects of free will is claiming personal power or rights. Stating that you are worthy or deserving and claiming material things is the physical reflection of claiming your spiritual reality. You are a spiritual being trapped inside a physical body. When you realize on a physical level that material things do not bring happiness, it opens physical doors within you that allow enlightenment to enter.

Even though you have toppled from the mountain of material endeavors, you may still be caught in the money trap. It is a sad fact of the world you live in. We spoke of the money trap in Chapter 6. The intents in that chapter will help you recover from the fall.

It is very difficult for you to keep yourselves from jumping on the merry-go-round of materialization; that gold ring is so tempting. Big business propaganda is there urging you on seven days a week, twenty-four hours a day. Television, radio, billboards, posters, and telemarketers compete for your attention.

## Competition Energy

Competition begins playing a key role in your life at childhood. It is no longer acceptable to be just average. It has been ingrained in you to strive to be better than the next person and to have more than the next person does...to be the winner...to be the best. Competition energy seeks the sight of those outside you, looking at you. It is like a false presentation in your heart. It allows the heart to vibrate at a certain frequency where mental and physical energies are activated. But this kind of energy deactivates intuition, the inner knowing, the inner God Spark.

There has always been much controversy about this issue, even on the inner planes where we reside, because there has always been the desire of some to go to the peak and attain the highest achievement or reward, no matter what the cost. But this desire needs to come into balance. It is not nurturing your souls or your existence on the planet.

## Fear of Failure to Win

People who have been in top-notch athletic competitions soon come to know the outcome of their passion. They know how much effort it took to get where they are. Now they may be feeling unfulfilled in their lives. Powerful energies have been expended against others to keep them on top. Their bodies have been used like superior machines. Whether or not they win, they live under terrific pressure and compression on the perpetual edge of the fear of failure to win.

Their original passion for the sport they engaged in seems to have turned against them, keeping them focused on it alone and cut off from everything around them, including those they love. They find themselves alone and lonely, in a rut, in a cycle from which they cannot seem to escape. They need to be told, "You are now ready to take this intensity of trying to be the best and convert it into the Love vibration."

## Competition, an Electromagnetic Pattern

Competition seems to be an electromagnetic pattern that exists on your planet. We have found it in every system we have observed: business, athletics, education, politics, religion, the arts and sciences, health and human services—everywhere. It seems to appeal to the mental makeup of humans, especially the ego. You sometimes call it "the Jones syndrome," or keeping up with the Joneses. It eventually produces sadness, grief, pain, and professional jealousy.

Not everyone who reads our words will accept them and then change, but many will understand what is happening and will do the internal work to change this scourge of competition in their lives.

## The Mind Competing Against the Heart

Competition exists on subtle levels. It exists in the body itself, with the mind competing against the heart. It is imprinted in the fibers of your being. Everyone experiences it. Humans need to go into their cellular level and ask for God's loving light to be present where competition energy exists. Ask yourself to search out and weed out where these aspects of competition exist in your lives and in your families. Say with passion, "My intent is that the Light of Love be present in these competition areas."

Competition excludes. It is abusive. It does not unite. It is a serious problem that cannot be solved overnight. However, there is a solution, and it is beginning to happen. Love can transcend the negative aspects of competition. More

Love than ever before is coming onto the planet. The energy of competition is going to receive Love. Love's way is not to decrease the intensity of competition but to expand and fulfill it. People on Earth have to love that part of themselves and not in any way condemn it.

## Competition and the Ego

You have gone as far in competition as you can go. Competition and the power it spawns are destroying the Earth. People are numb to the fact that the Earth is being destroyed. The ego is running competition. The ego goes down into the heart, but it is a false god. The ego is afraid of being killed, but we do not want it killed. It needs to go to its right place. The ego needs some gentleness and compassion. It needs a space in which it is allowed to have a fit. In some people, the ego will rise up and lash out. Ego blinds you to the thoughts and feelings of others. It is the all-consuming self.

The dark star cousins imposed competition on you. They have written texts in secret on how to disempower people using competition. Its essence takes you out of who you are and makes you find a subject to compete with or against. A gap exists between those who feel good from winning and those who feel good when others win. People with heart need to help clear competition. They are the people who will identify with its unnatural pressure and will be happy to back off and find new ways.

## Start with the Children

The primary solution for eliminating competition and its destructive effects is to start with the children and help them to grow and develop without competition in their lives. This new generation of children has not been imprinted with competition. They can learn it only through the efforts of you, their parents, and society; through television; their schooling; and yes, even through their churches. Now it is time for a change.

This new generation of children actually finds themselves fighting the system. But they will be able to change more quickly than even their parents will. You who understand need to send blessings to these children, saying, "It's okay." Their hearts need support. Then you need to help these children find ways to bring Love into competition.

The dark cousins set up the idea of winners and losers and made Earth a world full of losers with a small number of winners. The winners were set up to separate themselves from the rest, to make them feel better than the rest. The Creator does not believe in this structure. This is not the structure of Love.

## Teach Children Differently

Children need to be taught differently about winning. If they can connect to the feeling of the winner, they can feel good inside. In the new age that you and they will help to create, there will be many races and many winners. Winners will not be attached to winning every time. They will understand that everyone wants a chance to win and that their connection to the feelings of different winners makes them feel just as good as the winner does. They will understand that there are many races, and if everyone does his best, there will be different winners every time.

These new children will also learn that even when they are playing on different teams, they are still on the same team. Their team may win on the first day, but another team will win another day. The joy they feel will be for engaging in something exciting together. Each team will strive to do its best, and one will win. Next time they meet, the other team may win. The

*Speed Bumps on the Road to Enlightenment*

team that does not win will still feel good because of their emotional connections with the other team. They, too, will experience the joy being felt by the winners.

## Win/Lose Concept Needs Changing

Sound impossible? It can happen if people on Earth begin with the children. Do not impose upon them your old ideas of winning and losing. Re-member that they are coming to Earth without carrying the imprint of competition. This means that they can be taught a new and better way to engage in games, races, and sports—in fact, in life itself. This new way will be just as exciting and fun for them, but without the painful feelings of losing and without the aim of putting down other people and making you the best.

The win/lose concept is one of the greatest losses on the planet. It is not an evolutionary concept. In the long run, the fun or joy of Spirit has been taken out of competition. It is almost as though the competitors are owned (as many are in professional sports), and the joy of competition has been taken away.

## Preschool Teachers Can Help

If parents have a difficult time instilling these new ideas in their young children, they may want to turn to preschool teachers. These teachers can lead activities or play games with their children in which everybody is a winner.

In the Ezra Jack Keats book *Pet Show*, for example, one preschool staff member in the story made sure everyone brought a pet. One boy brought an empty jar. When asked what was in it, he said, "A germ." Each of the pets won a blue ribbon for displaying some characteristic. There was the dog with the longest tail, the cat with the longest whiskers, the gerbil who ran around the most, the budgie bird with the bluest feathers. The germ was awarded a blue ribbon for being "the quietest pet." They all talked about what it felt like to win a blue ribbon and how the others felt.

## Can Everyone Win?

But what about races? Someone has to win, doesn't he? In another preschool, the teacher prepared a series of sticks painted different colors. Each day, the children determined which color would be first place in the race. The winner would receive that stick. The next day, that winner watched while another winner won and got another colored stick. By the end of the week, almost everyone had a colored stick. Each stick was a winning color, and almost everyone had been a winner. Finally, they were down to one last child. Everyone wanted her to win, and she could feel it. Of course, she won and got her colored stick. Then she, like the other winners, was able to have her say.

After every race, the teacher asked the winner to tell what it felt like to win. Then the other children tried to feel what that day's winner felt like and tell about it. Young children are more often able to pick up the feelings of others than adults are. These children could be, and rejoiced to be, a part of each winner's joy. They couldn't wait to hear what the winner had to say, because often they already felt the same way.

## What Winning Feels Like

The objectives of this race, and every other activity in that preschool, was that every child could be a winner, and the other children could get to feel what the winner felt like. Feeling what the winner felt like and talking about it became just as good as winning for these youngsters. Children who tried to talk about losing were reminded that the race was about winning, not losing, and everyone would have a chance to be a winner and tell about it.

Once young children have been exposed to such concepts, they accept them willingly. Few are willing to go back to the old ways, where one child could dominate and the others all felt bad. They did not want to participate in the old win/lose games. Parents were invited to the school to watch the races or participate in helping with other activities. If they could not come during their working days, they came to evening meetings or potlucks and heard the teachers talk about the new concept of winning. They even played a few simple table games and became winners themselves. The winners told the others what they felt like. Several said it was the first time they had ever won anything. Then the other parents were invited to tell how they felt about the winners winning.

## Play Winners' Games

These parents were encouraged to play winners' games with their children at home. Their children could teach the parents how to do it, if they forgot—how the winner gets to say what he feels like, and everybody else gets to feel it, too.

Some of these teachers went on to become group leaders for training the elementary teachers in the grades that their preschool children would be attending the next year. All were asked to participate in the new "feel-what-it's-like-to-be-a-winner" concept. If they forgot to put this concept into practice, the preschool children who came to their classes soon reminded them.

To the people of the planet, we say once more, you are *all* truly gifted! You just don't know it. The dark cousins have taken away some of your self-esteem, not wanting you to know your greatness. Now is the time to change. Look to your young children to lead the way.

To the teachers of young children, we have this to say, a teacher's greatest service is to allow his or her children to do their own thing. Janice has told you in her many early childhood textbooks how to set up your classroom into learning centers where children can become self-directed, pursuing activities of their own choosing and completing them successfully on their own.

## Discover Children's Inspirational Desires

Now, we say, there is a new paradigm for teachers—that is, discovering children's *inspirational desires*. This is a key phrase meaning where a person's passions lie. Even young children often express these desires in the activities they like best: their art, their constructions, their games, the stories they like to hear. These children will someday become the new artists, athletes, builders, mathematicians, writers, and scientists of the world. Helping children discover their inspirational desires, such as what activities appeal to them, helps them to be successful in their lives to come.

## Be a Bridge Builder

Your other big task, teachers, is to find new ways to incorporate the "winners' competition concept" into learning. If all were right with the world, competition and learning would have a bridge connecting them. You can help to build that bridge by helping your children to feel how the other person feels. Call it *other esteem*, if you want. Then take your own feelings and those of others into academic learning. It can be done. Open your heart, and feel how you would like to do things differently. Your children will help you.

In this book, there are major signposts on the road to enlightenment. Respond to any one of them seriously, and your lives will change. Re-member, teachers, you are not the great authorities you may think you are. Your children may know as much as you do without being able to express it because of their immaturity. But you can help them learn about themselves, about their behavior, and about learning. You can be great facilitators, building bridges to learning for your children. Open your hearts, and allow yourselves to feel how to do it. Then observe and listen to your children. Let them help you lead the way to a better world.

## You Are Not Alone

The emphasis on physical strength and material gain has overshadowed Spirit. You will notice that we said, "overshadowed." When you stand in darkness, the shadows surround you. But when you step into the light, you notice that your shadow is actually beside you—a companion. Shadow is to remind you that you are not alone. Instead of competing against others and standing as a solitary icon to success, you need to feel a sense of camaraderie with your fellow man. Do not stand as a lone tree, but become a part of the forest. Community offers support, strength, and encouragement and is a huge conductor of energy.

## The Buddy System

As you travel on your road to enlightenment, you study and try many things to gain knowledge. You often grow very impatient for things to happen. You want very much for the world to become that land of enchantment, that reflection of Home. It can be. But you have to reach outside yourself to make it so. The next time you pray or meditate for something, try the buddy system. When two people pray or meditate together, you establish polarity. The negative and positive energies begin to flow and rotate. The flowing energies become in sync with the circular rotation of Earth and universe. The energy flow between you creates a vortex that draws in that energy from the universe.

## A Buddy Exercise

- Sit on two chairs facing each other with knees and fingertips touching.
- Allow yourself to feel the energy begin to swirl around you.
- Once you feel this circular energy, begin your meditation or prayer.

## The Camelot Energy

When you share yourself with others, what you could not accomplish on your own manifests. The more people you gather into your circle, the more energy you draw. This is the ancient Camelot energy and the purpose behind the Round Table. If your group should compose one of the sacred numbers, such as 9 or 12, the potential for even greater energy will be there. Group meditations and prayers have accomplished many miracles. Group prayer has been proven many times to have a positive impact for healing.

Communal consciousness has also stalled armies and diverted catastrophes. The Camelot energy is upon you now. Portals are appearing everywhere and being noticed by many. You are closer than you think to stepping into the Fifth Dimensional realm of Camelot. Have patience a little while longer. The knights in shining armor are on the road again.

*Speed Bumps on the Road to Enlightenment*

The gate is open;
The dam is rift;
It comes to you
From the universe: a gift
And so it arrives…

CHAPTER 9

# Fasten Your Seatbelts

It is appropriate that we offer this information to you on the autumnal equinox. The fall of the year is the time of harvest. Your prayers are answered, and the fruits of your labor become manifest, more often in the fall than any other time of the year. The time between the autumnal equinox and the winter solstice is an open window through which manifestation flows.

## Be in the Right Place Physically

We hear you say, "My prayers haven't been answered. My wishes haven't been manifested." You have heard the saying, "being in the right place at the right time." This is the key to the manifestation of your dreams. Not only do you have to be mentally, emotionally, and spiritually at the right place, you physically have to be there, too. You may be spiritually at the right place where you can accept your dreams, but you also need to be physically in the right place where they can be played out. The windows are there. You created them. Your wishes and dreams are the manifestation of your contracts.

How many of you have experienced dramatic success in your life after a move? You placed yourself in the right path, and your window opened for you. It does not necessarily mean you have to move in order for your dreams to manifest. You may simply need to step out of the safe little box you have created for yourself. You may be so afraid of failure or heartache that you never take a chance on life. Often, all it takes for your dreams to manifest is for you to step outside that box of safety and say, "Okay, world, here I am."

## Why Hasn't God Answered My Prayers?

We hear many of you asking, "Why hasn't God answered my prayers, my wishes?" We say to you, do not look without, but within. Do not take out your frustrations on Creator, but look within to find that piece of yourself that is not quite ready to step into your dream. A great deal of anger has been built up around prayer, because it appears that Creator has not been there…that he has not answered many of the prayers directed to him. However, this is not the real case. Spirit has been blocked from the hearts of too many of you. You need to heal your hearts, to open the roadblocks that are preventing communication between you and your higher self. Spirit has been trying to get in even the smallest crack, because Spirit can ride on your prayers.

## See Yourself as Spirit Sees You

When you pray, you need to see yourselves as Spirit sees you. Too many do not. They come to prayers with feelings of unworthiness. They need to begin by saying, "I ask to see myself as I truly am." This will open cracks in the roadblocks and begin to let Love into their beings. Or you can say, "I ask to feel acceptance of the state I am in at the moment."

Many of you feel you have to cleanse yourselves before you show yourselves to Spirit. But this will not happen without Spirit's help. Instead, you often hide parts of yourselves from Spirit and hold little secrets in your hearts. Spirit will help you heal those parts—the perversion, the darkness. You are not the cause. You are not the cause. You cannot heal them by yourself. When you are being overly critical and condemning about yourself, ask that Love to exist in place of those thoughts.

## Allow Love to Ease Your Pain

When you say your prayers have not been answered, you are right. Prayers cannot be answered when your mind has done the asking. An outer circumstance cannot be healed without your being able to go into the pain at the core that causes this circumstance. Open your mouth, and let the pain come out. Cry. Make sounds of anguish. Let Earth's vibrations come into the sounds of your pain so loving light can find its way to your depths. Ask for help. Ask for light. Do not be afraid of your emotions.

Some powerful emotions may arise when you allow Spirit to go into your pain. Spirit's blessings may trigger emotions of which you were not aware. If you are overwhelmed by such strong feelings, ask that these emotions move to another place until they receive light.

You on Earth have learned wrong about trying to access Spirit through prayer. You have not allowed your natural connection of Love to emerge. Everything will become less dense on Earth when the Spirit of Love fills your heart, your mind, and your body. When you add a strong intent to your prayers, then a great transformation can take place on Earth. Intent to know the Spirit of Love will help both on an intimate, personal level, as well as on a global level. You must feel this Love in your body and your heart. Allow the Spirit of Love to fill your heart and mind, and your prayers will be answered.

## Have Intent to Feel Blessed

Spirit is sending out blessings to you, but you don't receive them. You need to have *intent* to feel blessed. Then anger will dissipate. Then you will feel Spirit's Love and the answers to your prayers. Say it aloud, and let it ring out on Earth: "I feel blessed today!" Can you feel it in your heart? Then intend in your prayers about others, "I want you to feel blessed today!" Your blessing will resonate in the hearts of you both.

Prayers for others, when offered from the heart, are powerful. When people die and pass over from your three-dimensional existence, prayers of Love really do help them go to their right places. If you had problems with such people in this life that didn't clear, you should seek resolutions, even partial resolutions. Ask Spirit to help. Here is a powerful mantra to use.

### Love Mantra

*I allow Love to love me where I need to be loved.*

*I allow Love to heal me where I need to be healed.*

*I allow Love to live in me, all of me, and all I encompass;*

*Where Love desires to live.*

Many people pray. If they would just add these simple intentions to their prayers, things would change on Earth.

## Warriors of the Light

For many of you, the road to enlightenment is a solitary one. You may have family and friends you love, but you are content with being alone. You live strong, independent happy lives without the need or desire for a partner. You are truly blessed that you are at the point in your life lessons where you have such confidence and comfort in yourselves. Relationships—good, bad, or indifferent—take lots of time and energy. You, our independent warriors of the light, are in for exciting times. You are the champions. Like the legendary Knights of the Round Table, you bravely step forward without fear and champion the cause of many. With humility, Love, and fierce determination, you get the job done.

Some of you may be famous, and others of you quietly tread your own path. Either way, you all make a positive impact. Mother Teresa was such an individual. We do not need to extol her virtues. You are already aware of her dedication. We are not saying we expect you all to become like Mother Teresa. She is merely an example of a warrior of the light—a solitary individual who impacted the lives of many.

In the light energy of the Aquarian Age, changes will occur rapidly. Situations and problems that took long periods to resolve in the old energy will turn around in the blink of an eye. Long-forgotten abilities will come rushing in like a flood. You, our solitary knights, will be there to coordinate and take charge of these rapid changes. There will be no room for boredom; you came into this life for just this purpose. So fasten your seat belts, and keep both eyes on the road ahead.

## You Are the Test Pilots

As you travel deeper into the Aquarian Age, you will need to keep yourself open to new concepts and abilities, for you will be the test pilots who will help and instruct the masses. Your

## Speed Bumps on the Road to Enlightenment

inner light will shine before you. Freedom from the distractions of relationships will enable you to touch the lives of many.

There are those of you who have been in relationships but now find yourselves confident and independent. Your time is upon you to carry the torch. Others of you carried the torch earlier in your lives. You were the seed carriers. You planted the seeds of knowledge in your travels and encounters, and now you rest in the comfort of your family, watching your gardens grow. Julie has some more information to share with you.

> **Julie's Story**
>
> I was one of those seed planters. I moved around a lot and touched the lives of many. Even during my first marriage, I was very independent. I often found myself with new friends with absolutely no knowledge of anything spiritual. Conversations with me were often the only source of religious or spiritual information they had ever had in their lives. If they did have some religious background, I happened to meet them when they were questing for more. I also met a lot of lightworkers, all manner of healers and visionaries. I became a link to bringing these lightworkers together. I have noticed we all carry a different piece of the puzzle of life.
>
> The people I met who needed information or healing that I was not able to provide I put in contact with a lightworker that I knew. Without even realizing it, I had set up a vast network of lightworkers all across the United States. It is only in retrospect that I noticed this. When I was living it, I did not see it.
>
> I re-member a time I was crying to my sister, wanting to know what my purpose on Earth was. She was the

> one who pointed out to me what I had accomplished. She told me I was like an advanced scout or pied piper who found the trail for everyone. Every time I took a detour on my road to enlightenment, I picked up tailgaters and led them back onto the main road. Even though they had made their own choices, I helped to establish a network of support for them. Until my sister pointed this out to me, I never realized the impact I had made in so many lives. This was the turning point that enabled me to recognize my own path, which helped me find the right place for my window to open.

## Blessed Are the Torch Bearers

Thank you, Julie. That is a wonderful life, isn't it? How many of you have seen the movie *It's a Wonderful Life*? It is truly a story inspired by spirit. In this respect, life is like the movie. You do indeed impact every life with which you come in contact. Even brief encounters can have a profound effect. This is why you are called "warriors of the light." You bring your light into even the smallest space.

Sometimes, the light you carry can seem a burden, the weight of it hard for you to bear. But the Spark inside burns strong, and even though you may falter, you cannot give up. When you think you can go not one step further, you muster a determination from deep inside. You do what has to be done no matter what. Blessed are the torchbearers, for they shall bring the light.

You, our solitary warriors of the light, are old and wise souls. Your connections to Home are strong, and your knowledge banks are full. Even though you wear the veil of humanity, it does not cloud your steps. You carry the strength and knowledge of ages within you.

## Janice's Purpose

Janice, you are one of these wise souls. You brought to light the way for the education of indigo and crystal children. The "old structure" of learning was too harsh for these gentle souls. In the old structure, individualism was frowned upon. Your books, Janice, advocate and encourage self-expression in these wise souls. You guide teachers to respect the students and the students to respect one another. "Respect" is the steppingstone to Love and becomes the cornerstone to building a new world. We thank you, Janice, for all you have done and for what you will continue to do.

Even when life has been a burden, almost too much to bear, you found the inner strength to keep you going. We know the pain your separation from Dale has caused you. It was not planned. It was a "bleed-through." You are a very old soul, and your veil is very thin. When you met Dale, you were overcome with past life emotions, a "bleed-through." You had much contact at night with your soul group during your years with Dale, so they could assist you. You were very adamant that you could handle it, even though you knew it would be short-lived. Much Love was and is being sent to you.

When someone has a past life bleed-through, they experience twice the emotion. The emotional memories of the past and present lives merge. A bleed-through is like a tear in the fabric of time. It can be mended, but whatever leaks through becomes a part of you. So, Janice, it was not a sadistic act perpetrated on you by your higher self or anyone else. It was an accident. You and Dale would have met regardless, but the emotional attachment would not have been the same. We hope the joyful memories of the time you spent together outshine the sadness. You are truly a warrior of the light.

## Let Go and Let Spirit Take Charge

We say, allow your heart of hearts to see beyond the veil of negativity. Let the Spirit within take charge. Let your Spirit guide you. If your life is not going in the direction you want it to, then you need to change lanes. If you go through life always in the passenger seat, you will never get to where you want to go. You need to take charge of your life. Climb into the driver's seat. Fasten your seat belt, and go.

It may be a wild ride. You might find yourself going all over the road or even backwards. But eventually, you will find that you can assume control. Re-member, life and time are a circle. Past, present, and future coexist. It is the now. You may think you are going backwards and away from your goal, but in reality, you may be speeding faster toward your destination. Like your early explorer, Christopher Columbus, you can get to the East by sailing west.

## Prepare Yourselves for a Wonderful Ride

Earlier, we mentioned wrong perception. Things may seem negative. You may perceive a situation as negative when in reality, it is a clean slate for you. Many of you may be in grave and desperate situations. You have been brought down to the bare bones of existence. Prepare yourself for a wonderful ride. You have cleared yourselves from the last remnants of your karmic obligations and are on the threshold of a new energy pattern. Great things are about to happen.

Julie has a question: "I went through the poverty cycle and change of location two years ago, just prior to my re-marriage. Why am I experiencing the poverty cycle again?"

Thank you for this question, Julie. We hear this same question on the minds of many. As you are aware, this is the time when karma is ending. You ended a karmic relationship before you married, but you still had to end a karmic tie with your current husband. You are at the point now where you are stepping into an exciting new time without karmic attachments. The slate is clean for you to write your future. Do not be discouraged by the current state of affairs. Your higher self and the universe will provide. Allow the miracle to happen.

## Repetitious Life Patterns Are Ending

You all must re-member that you have many karmic ties in each lifetime. As each karmic relationship is ended, there will be some sort of adjustment period. Not only do you have karmic ties that are ending, you also have life patterns of repetitious behavior that are ending. When you end repetitious behavior patterns, you make space for newer, more positive things to enter. Old patterns and belief systems are rapidly disappearing in the new energy of the Aquarian Age. Your body, mind, and spiritual vibrations have changed.

The Aquarian energy is much lighter, and the Earth and your bodies are adjusting. The less dense you become, the greater your light will shine. The advent of the Aquarian energy heralds your entry into the Fourth Dimension. The Fourth Dimension is the transitional stage from Third Dimensional density to Fifth Dimensional light body.

## Mother Earth Is Changing

As you are going through personal life changes at a rapid pace, Mother Earth is changing also. You have witnessed these changes over the past several years. As the magnetics and vibrations change on Earth, you are experiencing more and more erratic weather patterns. Seasons are delayed or come early. Areas that usually have limited rain are having floods. Excessively long dry spells and abnormally high winds have triggered numerous forest fires globally. Lakes are shrinking, and oceans are expanding. The polar ice caps are melting, and migratory animals are appearing in areas where they have never been before.

The changing magnetic fields affect not only migratory land animals, but also the sea mammals. Look at the number of whales and dolphins that have been beaching themselves. Set a compass out where you can check it every day. There has been much fluctuation in magnetic north. One moment, it will read true; the next moment, it will read south or west. Earth changes such as quakes and volcanoes will be on the rise. You have heard this before.

## The Veil Is Becoming Thinner

As you are transitioning through the Fourth Dimension, an amazing event is occurring. The veil is becoming more like lace—patches of density with holes of light. You are able to catch more than a passing glimpse of the other side. Things that you used to think you saw out of the corner of your eye are staying visible much longer. These sightings are unsettling for some and downright scary for others.

A lot of you who are traveling on the road to enlightenment think of it as merely a fantasy or a curiosity. But as the veil thins more, you are coming face-to-face with reality. These slaps in the face by reality cannot be ignored. They are purposely tangible so that you cannot explain them away.

Many of you have been attuned since birth. You accept these things as fact and joyfully await the next event. But many of you need to be jolted out of your lethargy. Closed minds need to have physical proof that there is much more to the world around them. Startling events are needed to unlock those stubborn doors. Once the doors are opened, things will come through like a flood, and they will be impossible to shut. You may be able to stem the flow from time to time, but once the dam of knowledge is breached, you will be in for the canoe trip of a lifetime.

## The Canoe Trip of a Lifetime

Knowledge is not the only thing to come flooding in. When you are finally in your right spot, your dreams of a lifetime will come in one fell swoop. Julie will share her story as an example:

> From the time I was a young girl, ten or twelve years old, I had the same wish or dream for my future. This is what I used to say out loud all the time—"I want a husband, a home of my own, and a family. I don't care if I'm rich, just enough to be comfortable." In my twenties, it didn't manifest. I was married, but I knew, even before my wedding day, that it was temporary. We were both wounded people and needed to support each other. We divorced when I was thirty. My thirties were turbulent at best—emotional highs and lows still haunted by the demons of my past. I buried my needs and took care of others, moving from place to place, one step ahead of my insecurities.
>
> When I hit thirty-nine, I finally faced my fears. I confronted my inner demons. I confronted the people from my past who had abused me. I stepped off the familiar path of self-hatred and guilt, and I tried a new path of self-love and forgiveness. When I finally loved myself, I was able to draw true Love to me. I entered into a wonderful relationship with John. I moved to his home in November 2001. (I placed myself in the right place physically.) We were married a month later on the winter solstice, December 21, 2001. Five weeks later, on February 2, 2002, we gained custody of his

> brother's three children. Within a three-month time span, my dreams of a lifetime came true: a husband, a home, and a family. For the first time, I was mentally, emotionally, spiritually, and physically in the right spot.

Thank you, Julie. We hope that your story will help others to keep faith that their dreams will also come true.

## Forgiveness and Love Are the Cornerstones

We talked to you in chapter 4 about forgiveness and its importance. As you read in Julie's case, her happiness did not manifest until she had forgiven her abuser and come to terms with the life she had chosen for herself. Yes, re-member, you all chose the circumstances of your life. This is a hard truth for some of you to accept; but once you embrace your choices, your lives will change for the better.

Forgiveness and Love are the cornerstones in the foundation of your dreams. When you lovingly accept and embrace the life lessons you have set for yourself, your miracles begin to materialize. The speed with which they can arise is testament to the fact you are in the correct lane on the road to enlightenment. Once the roadblocks and your misconceptions have been cleared out of the way, you will need to fasten your seat belts, for your dreams will be approaching at warp speed.

*Speed Bumps on the Road to Enlightenment*

## The Great Cosmic "Two"

You might ask why we have cautioned you to fasten your seat belts. When you get into your cars, you fasten your seat belts in preparation for the unexpected. That is what we are preparing you for—a trip into the unexpected. Changes are occurring even as we speak. It is up to you as to how you will handle the ride. The only outcome we can predict with certainty is that the Earth will continue its evolution into the Fifth Dimension. This great event has been awaited and talked about for years.

But another great event made its entrance in the year 2000. The year 2000 was the advent of the Great Cosmic Two. Those of you who have studied numerology know that the number "2" symbolizes the feminine and duality. The age of the Cosmic One ended in 1999. The number "1" represents the masculine. It was the age of the aggressive survivor. The advent of the Great Cosmic 2 will enable Mother Earth to fully step into her contract as the harmonizer of the universe. When Mother Earth enters the Fifth Dimension, it will trigger not only a global change, but a universal one as well.

*You cannot affect this change. It is going to happen regardless.* What you can affect is your own change. If humanity can embrace the light within and start respecting the Earth and each other, it will be a smooth transition. But if you continue in your disrespect, it will be a bumpy ride with much loss. A great many of you are choosing to leave now. You will return to life after the transition. Your Love and prayers from the other side will aid those warriors of the light who are working through the shift.

## Love Affects Earth Changes

There was much talk about Earth changes prior to the year 2000. Aspects of these events still hold true. Modern-day prophets envisioned maps of what the new world would look like. Those maps were possibilities and could still be possibilities. Your ability to raise the Love vibration on Earth will affect the outcome of these changes. Some of you looked at those maps and moved to so-called "safe places." Your intent was to survive at all costs…to live through the transition. But for many of you, your contracts are "not to stay."

## Soul Fragments of Mother Earth

In the beginning of this book, we talked about contracts and soul groups. We told you how the original souls sent aspects of themselves to incarnate on Earth. Many of these aspects came from the soul of the Mother. The first children, the first man, were literally born of the Mother. Before embodying the Earth, the soul of the Mother split off a portion of herself to inhabit her later. Humanity is ever the reflection of Mother Earth. The soul of the Mother entered the Earth, and it has been in a sleep mode. The Earth has functioned not unlike your bodies function when you are asleep. But the Great Awakening is at hand.

Those of you who have contracted not to live through the transition are the soul fragments of Mother Earth. When you leave, you will merge again with the Mother to increase her energy for the age of the feminine. This is neither a sacrifice nor a death. It is a birth. Mother Earth is giving birth to herself. Our excitement is great on our side of the veil, for the awakening of the Mother will truly create heaven on Earth. The veil will disappear, and the lines of communication will be open. Loneliness will no longer exist. You will be able to see, feel, and re-member your connection to all things.

*Speed Bumps on the Road to Enlightenment*

We say again, fasten your seat belts, but not out of fear. Fasten them in anticipation of a wonderful ride. Like a giant movie screen, watch the road unwind before you, and enjoy all the beauty coming your way.

*Fasten Your Seatbelts*

## *Speed Bumps on the Road to Enlightenment*

All your dreams
At once come true:
Instructions missing
On what to do;
And so, it is overwhelming…

CHAPTER 10

# Help, I Got What I Wanted: What Do I Do With It?

You are the chefs of your destiny. You control your abundance and the surprises in your life. You write your contracts and toss them into the mixing bowl. You add a pinch or two of spice, a healthy dose of humor, and a bucket of tears to hold it all together. Then you wrap it in love and place it in a slow-cooking oven.

As it rises, it simmers and bubbles. If you try to hurry it along, it falls, or boils over and burns. You are smoked out and have to start from scratch again. But if you nurture it, take it slow, and allow all the ingredients to meld, the result will be a creative masterpiece. Then, at the perfect moment, you pierce the crust, and manna starts flowing forth.

You say, "Wait a minute. I only wanted one slice. I wasn't prepared to eat the whole pie." But there it is, laid out before you in all its succulent glory. You have taken that first slice of life, and you cannot put it back. The juices are flowing and will no longer fit back under the crust.

Such are your dreams. You mix in all the ingredients: happiness, sadness, wonder, mystery, surprise, despair, and achievement. You hold it all within you. Then comes that day when the dam breaks, and it all comes rushing out. "Now what?" you ask. We hear you saying, "Help! I got what I wanted." So what do you do?

## You Control Your Destiny

Re-member. You created it all. You can control it all. Instead of running in a panic and calling to the universe for help, take a deep breath and relax. This is your dream. Change it. Modify it. Take control of the gear lever, and shift it into low. Rejoice in the fact that you are in your right spot for your dreams to manifest. Don't let them run you over.

Your spiritual self becomes so overjoyed with the flow of manna from the universe that it forgets that it exists in a human body. The human mind can be overwhelmed when too much comes at it all at once. The instinctive survival mode of fear sets in, and the windows of communication slam shut. Julie will share more of her story as an example.

> **Julie's Story**
>
> I told you in the last chapter how I became wife, mother, and homeowner all at once. Well, it didn't end there. Not only did my husband John own his own home, but it came as part of a working farm, a family farm. Yep, that's right. Not only was I a wife and mother, I became a farmer also. Along with the farm, I also inherited a large dysfunctional family.
>
> John and I are very spiritually grounded and soon became the life preservers that kept the family afloat. We held steady a long time, but being human started

*Help, I Got What I Wanted: What Do I Do With It?*

to outshine being spiritual. Stress and fear began to take its toll. We were beginning to wobble with the stress, but the floodgates remained open, and manna was still flowing forth. All my dreams I had ever uttered were manifesting one by one.

I love to cook and feed people. I had always said I would love to feed at least fifteen people every week. You got it! During the week, I was feeding at least eight or nine people every night and twelve to fifteen people every weekend. I had quit my job when we got the kids so I could be there for them through the adjustment period. As a result, our resources were dwindling rapidly. I was entering into panic mode and starting to curse myself for ever wishing for these things.

By fall, things had started to settle into a routine, and I decided to look into taking a training course of some sort, something I had always wanted to do. A class on becoming an entrepreneur presented itself, and I signed up. The class project was to write a business plan on a business you would like to open. Needless to say, I not only wrote the business plan for a New Age bookstore and café, I submitted it to a local bank. Against tremendous odds, I got the loan.

**When Fear Settled In**

By December 1, I was in business for myself. Spirit helped pave the way. Everything I needed for my business seemed to leap right at me. It was simple... too simple. The first few months were good. Then things started to slow down. What little we had left at home, I funneled into the business. I began

> thinking like a human and allowed fear, despair, and hopelessness to settle in. The more despairing I allowed myself to be, the worse my business became.
>
> Now, I consider myself an enlightened individual. I have read all the books and have counseled many people in the belief that you get what you project. I know how it works. If you fear and worry about something, that is what you will receive. If you project negativity, you will receive negativity. I built huge negative energy walls around my business of anger, fear, and despair. I played at meditations, cleansing rites, and positive intents, but I never truly felt them. I was too caught up in feeling sorry for myself. Until I changed my attitude, nothing seemed to work. When I fell into thinking and acting like a human, I lost touch with my positive spiritual self.
>
> I finally got over my case of "poor me" and truly stepped into my intent, allowing Spirit to guide me. At this point, I was able to begin turning things around. I had waited thirty years for my dreams to come true, and I had let them consume me. My dreams are still manifesting. My window is still open. But now I control the flow. When things get a bit too much, I say out loud, "Okay, that's enough for now." I bless it, accept it, and thank the universe for it. Then I allow myself to adjust and absorb. I continue saying "thank you" until I am ready for more. My greatest advice to you readers is don't think like a human. Think like the powerful spiritual beings that you are.

Thank you, Julie, we could not have said it better ourselves. Being human does not have to be a handicap for you. On the contrary, being human allows you to experience many things that you could not experience otherwise.

*Help, I Got What I Wanted: What Do I Do With It?*

## Your Sexual Energy

One of the greatest gifts you humans carry within yourselves is your sexuality—sexual energy. Have you ever wondered why energy is associated with sex? It is because your sexual energy acts like a battery re-charger. Sex stimulates your root chakra and enhances your connection to Mother Earth and Home. Your sexuality has a vibration and frequency that recharges and balances you. Like taking your car for a tune-up, sex enables your body to function more smoothly.

When the cares of the world are getting the best of you, and stress is eating away at you, making love or releasing pent-up sexual energy can be an amazing curative. But often when stress overcomes you, sex with your partner is the first thing you shut down. Maintaining a good sexual connection between partners during stressful times will help channel new energy into the situation.

## What If You Don't Have a Partner?

What if you don't have a partner? Then you need to explore your own sexuality. Let your body talk to you. Experiment with caressing yourself. Your body will guide you. Release your guilt about sex along with your stress. Strive to forget the mankind-imposed strictures of morality. Re-member, in your true essence, you are, at the heart of yourselves, androgynous beings. That is, you encompass both male and female attributes. To pleasure yourself is a sacred right, not a mortal sin.

You humans surround yourselves with many things that emit sexual vibrations without even knowing it: washing machines, lawn mowers, vacuum cleaners…anything powered by a small motor emits a sexual vibration. Sex toys are frowned upon, but it is perfectly all right to mow your lawn for five hours. Sexual vibration does not have to be orgasmic to be effective. Sexual vibration opens the sexual energy channels necessary for your health and well-being. It is part of who you are.

How many of you, when feeling stressed out, frustrated, or angry, go for long drives in your cars? The motion of the wheels on the pavement, along with the engine, is a sexual vibration. It has the power to calm, soothe, and reconnect you to your spiritual self. Sexual vibrations are all around you. They are in the vehicles you drive, the music you listen to, and in the pounding of the surf. There are sexual vibrations all throughout nature. Mother Nature is herself a sexual being, and the vibrations within nature help to keep her balanced.

## The Roadblock of Sexuality

You need to step out of the Dark Ages and bring your sexuality into the light. Your sexuality has been a part of you since birth, and it does not serve you to deny it. Sexuality has become another huge roadblock for the human race. Most people have never truly understood their sexuality, nor has society or religion helped them in this regard. Thus, many people have hidden sexual secrets trapped in this energy. The magnetic energy that is trapped in the lower energy centers of the body, the lower chakras, causes a great deal of pain and suffering in the human species and throws up a huge roadblock on the road to your enlightenment.

People's unwillingness to confront their hidden secrets is not all their own doing. Followers of the dark star cousins have long controlled this energy. It contains ancient patterns of suppression of sexual abuse, fathers against their children, mothers with sexual secrets, perversions, rape, and every sort of erotic action that would bring shame to the perpetrators or victims. Even human DNA contains this code of silence.

Pain and suffering are continually going on in hidden places of your body because of your inability to confront these secrets. Most of the pain is stuck, hidden, never to be

## Help, I Got What I Wanted: What Do I Do With It?

uncovered. The magnetic energy that is created is like a dark dot—an implant of silence.

At this time, spiritual beings are looking at this problem in the human race. More and more of the hidden sexual secrets are being uncovered and brought into the light. But they are still being used and manipulated. The dark forces are in a frenzy over what is happening and are scrambling to gain control again.

Sexual arousal is part of human nature from birth until death. How people deal with it makes an important difference in their lives. If you deny sexual arousal because you are horrified by it, it remains trapped in hidden areas, thus magnetically empowering forces of unloving light to control it. This discussion itself may make you feel distaste or disgust, but it is necessary in order to bring the Light of Love into this darkness.

## Sexuality, the Legs of the Body

Do you feel that your genitals are as holy as your heart? Think about it. People need to bring the Creator's light into their orgasms. Nothing will be healed until this light goes all the way down to the root energy chakra at the base of the spine. The Light of Love should be as bright there as it is at the top of your head.

Janice asks us, "What is sexuality?" We say that it is the generator of life. Without sexuality, there would be no life. Sexuality is also a part of the Spirit of Love. It is truly the Love of life. Sexuality is the powerful legs of the body. How can the brain and heart function without the legs? Sexuality is why humans exist. But the denying of sexuality as a part of Love has to stop. Living things on Earth were produced by sexual energy. Give thanks for it. Allow the Spirit of Love deeper into your sexuality.

## Allow Love into Sexuality

There are people, of course, who know deeply that the Love they generate with sexuality generates Love for the planet, and they are actively doing this. But many people separate Love and sexuality. What this means is that they are separating the Creator from sexuality. The separation of the Creator in sex is causing wars. Yes. There is an incredible denial of the intensity of sexual energy going on. This denied and suppressed sexual energy must express itself somewhere, and it has the power to do great damage. How does this power manifest itself? In violence.

Many people are afraid to allow Love into their sexuality. People think that if they allow Love in, they will not have the intensity. The truth is that they will have more intensity in their sexuality than before. When you steal it from another, you have denied it within yourself. A great deal of sexual abuse happens because people do not have partners with whom they can experience sexual intensity.

Everyone has a sexual life whether it is open or secret. Sexuality is so powerful it has to be expressed in human beings from birth until death, either openly or secretly. Many people are confused by the darkness of their sexuality and the secret world they inhabit with it, but they don't have the power to change it. Yet the condemnation they have on themselves is worse than the darkness. Even people with good hearts have judgments against their sexual feelings. Now is the time to lift guilt off sexuality in order to allow in Love.

## Release Guilt about Sexuality

Were you taught to feel guilty about sex as a child? Now is the time to release this feeling. The Spirit of Love wants to come into it. It is time to release the self-condemnation you feel.

## Help, I Got What I Wanted: What Do I Do With It?

Be sure, though, to accept your own children's sexuality. They should not learn to feel guilty about it.

You cannot invalidate the guilt you have about sexual energy. Instead, honor it. It cannot be released all at once. But you can forgive yourself for having believed you were bad for having held secret sex fantasies for so long. Many people's sex fantasies take the form they do, not from their own choice, but because of something that happened to them earlier, perhaps in another life. So forgive yourself. Tell yourself you are not bad, but mistaken. It is possible to have appropriate sexual fantasies by changing them in a positive way. Then the dark dot, the implant of silence, will shift and vanish.

## Letting Go of Fears

You hold many fears about your sexuality. In fact, you hold many fears about lots of things. Fear is one of the top five roadblocks on your road to enlightenment. Those of you who have made great progress on your road to enlightenment think that you do not have fears. If you step back and really examine yourselves, you will find that you hold many fears. These fears can affect you mildly or be completely debilitating. You may be an enlightened individual in how you relate to others, but if a mouse or spider were to cross your path, fear would take over. These kinds of fears spark different reactions in people. Some of you may simply freeze on the spot and be rendered mindless in terror. Others will scream and run. The rest of you will go into battle mode and search for the most convenient implement to send the object of your fear back to Creator.

### *Common Fears*

Many different reactions can relate to a common fear. Fear of animals, fear of insects, fear of water, fear of heights, or fear of fire often have their roots in cellular memory. They are triggered by past life memories in which you experienced harsh survival times or died in cataclysmic events. Fear is a side effect of your survival instinct. Fear became more pronounced in your biology when the dark cousins tampered with your DNA. When you lost your telepathic abilities and were unable to communicate with the animal and nature kingdoms, fear and violence were born on both sides. As you gained enlightenment about the environment around you, you made much progress in resolving these kinds of fears.

## *Emotional Fears*

Many of you have emotional fears. You fear Love or become jealous. Yes, jealousy is triggered by a fear of something lacking in you. If you truly believed in yourself, you would not be jealous of qualities you see in others. For example, people who hold professional jealousy about someone often lack confidence in themselves. When people are jealous of others who have money or wealth, they are expressing a fear of abundance. In other words, they do not feel they deserve wealth.

## *The Greatest Fear*

Lack of faith is the greatest fear of all. Even though Spirit tells you often just to have faith and things will work out, you still fear and doubt. The fear of placing your faith in something has roots at the very beginning of your life cycles. When the dark cousins were warring for supremacy over you, they presented themselves as gods. These false gods asked you to trust in them, believe in them, and have faith in them. You did, and they did not reciprocate. You were burned on faith, and your fingers are still stinging. You need to re-member your true connections to Creator and the angelic realm. The following exercise will help you to clear yourself of fear.

*Help, I Got What I Wanted: What Do I Do With It?*

### Releasing Fear

- Take a deep breath, and blow it out.
- As you blow out, tell yourself that you are blowing away the illusions of fear.
- As you breathe in again, tell yourself you are filling yourself with Love and Divine connection.

(Repeat this exercise three times.)

## Faith as Co-Pilot

Open yourself to the experience of true faith. Allow the breath of divine life to propel you on your road to enlightenment. Release your fear of faith, and fully embrace life. Allow faith to be your co-pilot, and it will never steer you wrong.

There are more blessings and more Love radiating out from the Source of Love and coming to people on Earth every day than you are open to receive. The receptors on your road to enlightenment have been blocked. When you start opening these roadblocks to allow this Love and to receive the blessings that are already there, they don't just stop inside of you. They flow through you and out to others. But some people with busy and often chaotic lives need to do more than simply stop. They need to participate in a rite that will put them in touch with themselves and the Creator. We call it *ritual*, and we are asking Janice to write about it.

## What Are Rituals?

The term *ritual* is sometimes an uncomfortable one for people of the Western world. Perhaps you think it connotes some sort of strange rite practiced by indigenous people. If this is how you feel, you can substitute the word "ceremony," although to me a ceremony is more of a formal observance, done for a particular celebration such as a wedding. Rituals can be more informal rites and can be done at any time for any occasion.

The rituals we need to consider here are observances practiced for the purpose of deepening our connections with Spirit. A ritual can be practiced privately by an individual or with a group of people for the purpose of making a request, honoring a person, celebrating a milestone, dedicating a life, affirming a belief, asking for help, giving thanks—for almost any intent that requires the attention, assistance, or blessing of Spirit. Rituals are personal expressions of our relationship with the sacred.

A ritual affirms what we believe and offers us a focus for this affirmation without the distractions of the world around us. It is a pause or a stepping aside from our daily lives to contact the spiritual world. It affords a time and space for safely expressing deep emotions. We shift our perspective of our conscious existence and try to connect with something deeper within us. Ritual is, in fact, the principal tool for approaching the unseen sacred world.

## Where Should You Practice Rituals?

"Rituals can be practiced anywhere you feel secure: a particular location in your home, in your car, in your office, in a park, in your garden, at a burial site, by the side of the road, in a meeting room, in a grove of trees, by a flowing river, or whatever site to which your heart is drawn for the purpose of approaching the sacred. Sometimes a particular spot is chosen because people feel that its beauty or energy is especially inspirational.

*Help, I Got What I Wanted: What Do I Do With It?*

## What Is Included in a Ritual?

Most rituals, whether impromptu or planned, include some sort of opening or *invocation*—for example, a prayer or chant that formally invites Spirit to be present. Next comes the expression of your *intent* that may use words, singing, meditation, or even dancing, drumming, or drama to allow the content and emotion of your purpose to reach Spirit. Finally, there is a *closing* in which you express your gratitude and give thanks for receiving the blessings of Spirit. Be sure to give thanks for the help, healing, or protection for which you have asked. Once again, affirm your beliefs. You may want to close with a mantra repeated several times.

It is not necessary to use words, although most people do. Some people pray silently. Words, on the other hand, can clarify your intentions. The words can be those you make up on the spot or be memorized words made up by others. They can be prayers, chants, poems, or songs. Whatever you use, try to feel the energy of your soul in them. Words can be magical, evoking emotion and the Spirit of Love. They can be doorways to the unseen world of Spirit.

Sometimes in a ritual, it is necessary to move physically in order to move emotionally. Music and dance can help you accomplish this. Prescribed dance steps are not necessary. You may simply want to move around, wherever your body or feet take you, to the song in your heart or the beat of a drum. It is difficult for many people to break through long-held inhibitions in order to dance. You may want to perform your rituals privately until you feel safe and free enough to express yourself among others.

## What Tools Do You Need to Perform a Ritual?

Tools are not necessary for performing a ritual, but they are also totally acceptable. Some people erect an altar or shrine in a special sacred place in their homes or gardens. What these consist of depends on the purpose for the ritual or the personality of the supplicant. Some people place flowers, candles, shells, stones, feathers, a cross, a picture or statue of a saint, the picture of a loved one, or a cup or bowl with water or wine on their altars. Something with great meaning can be a power object to clarify your focus. Lighting a candle or incense is a sacred act that calls attention to the Creator as well as providing a space for your prayers to be spoken or felt.

The space you provide for such an altar needs to feel right to you. Stand in the space with your feet apart and your eyes closed, and feel it out. Be aware of the energy you feel. Breathe deeply, hold it, and let it out slowly. Can you feel yourself being centered, balanced? Can you feel the warmth of Spirit filling you? Ask aloud if this is a good space for ritual. Listen and feel for an answer. If nothing happens, feel out another space.

## How Do Rituals Make You Feel?

Their physical expression is something that can lift you up, pulling your energy up. It is not necessary to understand what is happening, only to feel it. Such movement can open up channels within you so that energy can flow freely. It can shake you from the rigidity of a controlling ego that wants you to keep your status quo and to limit your spiritual growth. If tears come, let them flow. They will release energy that needs to leave your body.

*Help, I Got What I Wanted: What Do I Do With It?*

Social conditioning has taught men not to cry, that they will lose control or be ridiculed. But men need to express the strong emotions they feel of grieving, of happiness, of relief, just as women do. Crying over the passing of a loved one is a cleansing process that purifies the body. Rituals allow everyone to express these emotions. Perform them privately if need be, until you feel you can face others.

We need to be aware of the void of ritual on our planet, especially in the Western world. People have been discouraged from doing ritual. Ritual has gotten "a bad rap" by being associated with so-called primitive people. The dark star cousins have encouraged people to regard rituals as "pagan rites" or "devil worship." By keeping people from performing rituals, they have blocked yet another means for your making connection to Spirit. Rituals, in fact, bring you closer to God. People who feel the lack of God or the Spirit of Love in their lives can regain this connection through rituals.

## Are Church Services Rituals?

Church services may try to be rituals, but many are, at most, shallow attempts, like the sticking of a toe in the water. Real rituals are filled with emotion. Church services where people move their bodies in joyous swaying and clapping and lift their voices in loud rejoicing through song have captured the true essence of ritual. Too many people are satisfied with mediocrity in their lives. They do not even realize they are missing something.

Through rituals, you should be able to feel power in your body. You should feel protected and loved. Churches that focus on preaching hellfire and damnation actually damage the psyche by creating fear. Real rituals are vehicles for fueling Love. If you walk out of a church feeling Love flowing out of you, then you may be in the right church. But it is not necessary to go to church to experience rituals or God's love.

*Speed Bumps on the Road to Enlightenment*

Private rituals can be profound experiences that take you into your heart. You need to go deep enough within yourself to activate your emotions. Your heart will actually start resonating to a different beat during the act of profound ritual. The act of ritual releases you where you are caught up in your everyday experiences and resentments. Ritual activates the Love Source. It sends this energy force into your life to make things easier and less conflicted. Once you have started this Love energy flowing, you will find that your decisions will be obvious about which direction you should follow. You may suddenly have more connections with loving people in your life. Most important of all, you may find that you will be giving gifts of yourself to others.

### *A Ritual Technique*

*Invocation:* Invite the sacred Spirit you are addressing.

*Intent:* Give your purpose for calling on Spirit.

*Closing:* Express your gratitude and give thanks for assistance; ask that the Love energy go out before you.

*Acknowledgment:* Say with emotion, "I acknowledge that the Love energy I have generated has the power to change things in my life; to redirect me when necessary; to bring me different choices; and to cause coincidences to happen."

## Misconceptions

Thank you, Janice, for your inspiring description. Now, if we may, we would like to expand on the subject. There is a great misconception on your planet about ritual. It is often viewed as a pagan tool. Often, when you think of ritual, you envision sacrifice, blood rites, and depraved acts. In fact, this misconception, this ignorance, affects many. So-called pagan religions fill many with a sense of fear and invoke within

## Help, I Got What I Wanted: What Do I Do With It?

you feelings of hatred. Think a moment. Re-member when and where these negative emotions originated. They are the signatures of the dark cousins. If they are prompting you to fear and hate paganism, then maybe you should ask yourself why. Turn it around on them. Actually, the dark cousins fear and hate paganism.

In its earliest definition, "pagan" meant "rural citizen." Pagans actually live in harmony and honor Mother Earth. Their rituals honor the sun, moon, and stars—the heavens. They chart the phases of the moon to use in planting cycles. The earliest people on Earth were all pagans, including the Lemurians and Atlantians—your ancestors. The harmony of Earth, air, and sky was the only religion.

The present fear and hatred of anything pagan was instilled in you by the dark cousins. They know that if you were to re-member the pagan connection between heaven and Earth, their control would be finished.

To harm none and live in harmony with nature is the pagan/Wiccan way. Wiccans are also pagans, not Satanists. Followers of the black arts are followers of the dark cousins and have no place in true religion. Wiccans and pagans have been deliberately maligned so that the dark cousins could maintain control. Are we saying you need to become pagans? Not at all. All religions have truth in them. What you need to do is take fear and control out of your religion and replace it with pure Love. Let go of these misconceptions, and get to the truth of the matter. Do not let someone else's truth become your own. Allow your heart of hearts to see beyond the veil of negativity.

Embracing your sexuality and reintroducing ritual into your lives are wonderful tools in calming your being. Many things in life, both good and bad, can overwhelm you. You need to find the tool that works best for you. We are not talking about taking a pill or drinking a cup of tea or bottle of beer. These things only relax the surface, the shell. We are talking about things that calm the soul, the whole being.

## Meditation

Meditation is the greatest tool of all. When you truly become adept at meditation, it can lead you Home where self meets self. We see that meditation is difficult for many of you. You are surrounded by noise pollution. Finding a quiet place is nearly impossible for many. What you need to do is find a calming sound to override the discordant noise. You need to find something that resonates within your being.

You have access to all kinds of music and nature sounds in your technological world. Some of you may be drawn to the sounds of water, wind, or the heartbeat of a drum. Find something that calls to the core of your being, and listen to it as you relax. These sounds may cause images to appear in your mind. When you see these images, ask yourself if there is an aroma attached to them. There are all kinds of scents available to you. Find one to complement and enhance your inner music. Is it the tang of a salty sea? The musk of a deep forest? An intoxicating bouquet of flowers? Or the smell of a fresh-baked pie? Whatever it is, let it speak to you.

Take these tools with you to a favorite spot, and relax. Let your body breathe in the images your mind invokes for you. Before you know it, you are taking deep breaths to feed these images. You smell that forest. You taste that salt tang. And wonder of wonders, you are really breathing!

## Breathing

You humans have forgotten how to breathe. Your breathing reflects the shallow image of self that you have carried with you for so long. You have forgotten that every inch of you is alive. When you breathe, you need to send that breath all the way to your toes. Take a slow deep breath. Exhale slowly. Take another slow deep breath. Follow that breath in your mind all the way to your toes.

*Help, I Got What I Wanted: What Do I Do With It?*

Would it surprise you to know that you may have just participated in a meditation? In reading the last few paragraphs, if you shut out the cacophony of the outside world and focused on what self was doing, you experienced a meditation. If you visualized any of the things we described, or enjoyed a moment of true peace, you experienced a meditation. There are many stages or steps in meditation. If you were able to find a place of peace and quiet for even a moment, it was successful.

We hear many of you say, "I fall asleep when I meditate." Our answer is that sleep is the deepest form of meditation. Re-member, we told you that it is in the sleep/dream state that you travel Home. Do not replace that feeling of rejuvenation when you awake with feelings of guilt. Instead, smile and tell yourself how wonderful and stress-free you feel.

## Guided Imagery

Deep meditations are achieved through guided imagery. A facilitator will lead you through a series of images that lead you deeper within. The biggest roadblock for many of you is that you have lost your imagination. You cannot visualize these images. You are so constantly surrounded by vivid imagery that you have forgotten how to create these images in your own mind. You need to practice projecting images in your mind. If you need the tools of sound or senses to achieve this, all the better. When you include sound and smell into your mental imagery, you are taking your first step into "whole viewing." Eventually, with enough practice, you will be able to achieve deep meditation without the need for tools.

## Rainbows

Imagination is the bridgework on your road to enlightenment. It allows you to cross over physical impediments. Take a picture of a rainbow, or draw one, and place it on top of your head when you meditate. Rainbows are nature's bridges—a fantastical leap from one place to another. Build a rainbow bridge in your mind, and enjoy the trip. Let the colors of your rainbow soothe you, so you are able to enjoy your dreams of a lifetime stress-free. Re-member, help is only a dream away.

*Help, I Got What I Wanted: What Do I Do With It?*

*Speed Bumps on the Road to Enlightenment*

Peace and tranquility
Around you flows;
The Love of Creator
Inside you grows.
And so it is...

CHAPTER 11

# I'm Not There Yet, But I Can See The Light

Hi, my name is Julie. I am not an alcoholic, or a drug addict, and I am not crazy. I have started my own support group: Me in Support of Myself, for I am wonderful. If I am wonderful, then so are you all. I have shared fragments of my life with you throughout this book. Why, you may ask, would someone wish to share intimate secrets, joys, and shames with total strangers? Good question. I suppose, like anyone else who has ever shared intimate knowledge, it is for healing. Not just my own personal healing, but for others, even Mother Earth herself.

This book really is an autobiography of the human race. The examples of my life contained within this book, even though they are uniquely my own, are representative of events that have happened to many. If I have gained just one piece of knowledge in the odyssey of writing this book, it is that we are all an aspect of each other. The thread of life that connects all living things has a common origin. We are all pieces of the Source of Life. I am you, and you are I, and we are all one.

## This Is My Chapter

This last chapter is my chapter—our chapter. The group has left it up to me. Oh, now I have your complete attention. Humans. You have to love our insatiable curiosity. You want to know who they are. (The group) How did they contact me? Why did they contact me? Can it happen to you? Where to begin…

First, I want to thank the wonderful soul who was my mother for encouraging and allowing enlightenment in our home. She always had a thirst to know more, and she shared what she knew with my brothers and me. Next, I need to thank myself. For did I not contract with her to be my mother and mentor? Her love and fierce determination were the beginning.

I always had what I call "knowings." When I was having conversations with people, and the topics went into areas about which I was completely clueless, I would find myself answering questions or giving advice and just "knowing" that what I said was true.

Later, when I had a chance to research the topic, I found out that the information I had given was correct. I started doing this when I was in my teens. I trusted it was accurate. I never really put any thought into it or worried about it. It just was.

## My Awakening

The other areas of my life were total chaos and devastation, filled with depression, despair, and feelings of unworthiness. I was able to offer spiritual information or counsel others who were experiencing similar problems, but I never let the inner voice talk to me. In retrospect, I look back and think I had set up so many roadblocks and encouraged the veil to remain so thick, so that I would not awaken to my true potential until the time was right. I believe everyone with whom I was to work in the years to come was also ending his or her karmic ties. My awakening and theirs had to wait until we all could be in our perfect spots around the same time.

From the time I was around ten years old, I always wished that I were forty years old. A part of me knew that, at age forty, I would begin my true life. On some issues, I always listened to my inner voice. When it said I was supposed to move and where to move, I did—over thirty times, in fact! Within three months of every move, the reason for the move presented itself in someone I needed to help or get acquainted with. But it was not until I turned forty that the awakening and self-healing process began. Forty years of pent-up trauma, fear, pain, self-loathing, and depression do not go away overnight. I am still battling my demons.

## Receiving a Mantle

"When I first opened my business in 2002, I was riding pretty high for quite awhile. But by the middle of my first year, my insecurities were crowding in big time. My great escape from the world had always been books—all kinds of books. I had sat down in the back room of my store to read and had only read a few pages when I felt this amazing energy come through me. It coursed through my body like liquid fire. It felt like a warm blanket had been placed over my shoulders. The word that came to my mind was "mantle." Someone had placed a mantle on me.

The dictionary describes a mantle as a cloak or cape, sometimes used figuratively in allusion to royal robes of state, as a symbol of authority or responsibility. (I now believe I accepted the responsibility for writing this book long before I was born.) Along with the mantle, I felt the energy really heavy in my forearms. I just knew I was supposed to share this energy with somebody.

## Sharing the Energy

I immediately started calling my network of psychically attuned friends. Every number I tried was busy. I said to myself, "Focus, Julie! Who are you supposed to share this with?" I immediately got the name of my longtime friend Janice. This time when I called her, the phone rang. I explained to her what the new energy felt like and that I knew I was supposed to share it or send it to someone. Since Janice is a professional writer, I told her I thought I was supposed to send it to her to help her channel. (Actually, Janice channels on her computer.) I thought the energy was for her to tap into to gain insight into a book she was considering writing.

Janice put on her headset, so her hands would be free to type my words, and poised her fingers above her keyboard. After several moments, she said she was not getting anything. I told her I was getting the words "heart healing." Janice said it was from the title of a manuscript she had written with another friend. I ended up feeding her a whole page of information.

## I Was Channeling!

*I* was the one who was channeling! The energy was for me! Simple me, a nobody! Things like this don't happen to people like me, average and with no higher education. I did not realize until that moment that I had such a misconception of what channeling is. I thought it could only be achieved in an altered state, a mysterious voice coming out of an unconscious or hypnotized person.

I now realize that there are multitudes of people who are channeling: writers, artists, musicians, scientists. All you need to do to become a channeler is to open yourself to the possibility. Allow it to happen. Look back on the events of your life. Maybe you are a closet channeler like me. I had been hearing voices and seeing images my whole life. I thought I was just weird, not a channeler.

*I'm Not There Yet, But I Can See The Light*

## The White Sisterhood

But here I was—wide awake, with words not so much heard as felt. Images also appeared. I saw six guides, three on each side of me. They had their hands on my forearms. Janice got that this was why they felt so heavy, that they were holding onto me so the force of the energy would not blow me away. It came to me that the name of the group was the White Sisterhood. Many of you who have a metaphysical background have heard of The White Brotherhood. The White Sisterhood is the feminine aspect of that group. They are sometimes called The Mother Mary Group.

[The Group jumps in here to clarify that the White Sisterhood and The White Brotherhood have nothing to do with race. On the other side, all is energy. The insignificance of race is a human lesson. Inside, you are all one family, one light, and the highest expression of that light is "white."]

## That's Not All

When I felt the Group leave, I was left with a sense of peace. I felt honored for the experience and did not really think it would happen again. I said my goodbyes to Janice, closed my store, and went home. Surprise, surprise! They were not gone! They had my undivided attention for the forty-minute drive home. My mind was flooded with their words. I had dinner guests that evening, and I could not call Janice until after nine o'clock. As I was talking to her, it came through to me that they wanted us to write a book together. We made plans to talk again the next day.

I had only been at work a short time the next morning when I again felt the mantle draped over my shoulders. They gave me the title of the book we were to write (Speed Bumps on the Road to Enlightenment), a chapter outline, plus a page of information. The information they gave me was about forgiveness, something I needed to do in order to achieve total healing and open myself.

## Strong Energy

At the appointed time I was to call Janice, I discovered my phone was dead. I thought it must be the battery and used my other phone. After sharing my information with Janice, I went and purchased a new battery and a hands-free tape recorder that I could use to record the information when I was driving. I discovered that it was not the battery after all. The circuits in my phone had been fried! The tape recorder wouldn't work, either. The energy proved to be too strong to be recorded into an electronic device. I had to write it down first. There is much power in the written word. That's why when you do mirror work, communicate with your angels, or state your intent, you are advised to write down the words that are used.

The information continued to flow daily. I needed to do nothing special to prepare myself. All I had to do was sit down and pick up my pen. Except for the first page that I channeled directly to Janice, the rest of the information came in the order of the chapter outline they had given. Janice and I did not have to struggle to figure out how and where to put this information into a book. It was like the book was already written and was merely being dictated to us. We bounced around many theories about this, one of which was that our future selves had written it. Since we do exist in the past, present, and future, I am sure, indeed, this is not the first time we have written this book.

## Overcoming My Doubts

Being human and aware of how ego works, I had some doubts about the validity of what I was writing. Every time I had doubts, someone would come into my store asking me for advice or telling me about an experience they had that was pertinent to the material I had just channeled. These coincidental validations happened almost daily. Even with these Coincidences, I still worried that I was letting my own thoughts come through. But again, I had another fail-safe.

    For years, I have had a problem with arm and hand weakness. I have never been able to write more than a few sentences without my hand cramping or my fingers going numb. But when I channeled, I did not have this problem. When I took a break from writing the channeled material to write a note for one of my employees, the cramping was back again. As soon as I resumed the channel writing, the cramping disappeared. Spirit does work in mysterious ways.

## Changing My Life

Now that I have shared how this all started, I need to share with you how this channeled information has changed my life. From the beginning, the words resonated within me. Though much of the information was similar to other channeled material I had read, this seemed more complete and much easier to understand. The speed bumps and roadblocks they mentioned were chapters out of my own life, which I shared with you. But emotions and images that their words created in me were awe-inspiring. I ran hot and cold with emotion. Happy. Sad. Confident. Anxious. Excited. Often, my mood would change by the moment. Not hours or days, but moments. I would say that the majority of the emotions that came up were negative. What a wonderful thing to finally express and release all that trapped garbage!

*Speed Bumps on the Road to Enlightenment*

## What Makes Happiness?

I recall my last negative day. I was feeling sad, depressed, angry, and lonely. You name it—if it was oppressive, I was experiencing it. I had some friends visiting me at my store that day. Even their company did not lighten my mood. One of my friends asked me, "What would it take to make you happy?" I just sat there with a blank look on my face. I could not answer her. After several minutes, the only thing that came to mind was being able to spend more time with my best friend Wendy, who lived in Maine.

I left for home a few minutes later, and it was as if someone had flipped a switch—all my dark thoughts had disappeared. I felt wonderful. Happy. Content. Worry-free. That day was several months ago, and I still feel the same. The reason for the change never entered my conscious mind until I started writing these last paragraphs. I realized that having more money, less bills, or increased business for my store would not bring me happiness. In the big picture of my life, those things meant nothing. What was the source of my happiness? Love. Simply Love. Being able to spend time with the people I loved was the key to my happiness.

When I realized my heart's desire was to be home with my family, everything fell into place. I had realized my heart's dwelling place. I am a nurturer by nature. I love caring for my loved ones and for Mother Earth. I no longer worry about money. I realize if you are doing what makes you happy, Spirit will provide. For me, home is where my heart is. What makes me happy may not be what makes you happy. But if you are doing something that brings joy into your being, Spirit will pave the way.

## Closing My Business

I made the decision to close my business, and within minutes, the money started flowing in. It was my confirmation that I had made the right choice. Some of you may wonder at this seeming fickleness of Spirit, for I told you earlier in the book how Spirit had paved the way for me to open this business. I do not feel that the path here has been a failure, nor do I feel Spirit set me up to fail. My first and foremost intent for my business was to draw out and meet the other metaphysically inclined people in the community. I knew there were many out there like myself, waiting to step out of the shadows, like the line from the movie *Field of Dreams*: "If you build it, they will come." And they did.

I started a discussion group called "The Circle of Light," and that's what we have become. People who had lived next to each other all their lives discovered they were "light thinkers." Yes, I meant "light" and not "like." Our Circle of Light has reached across religious and social prejudices into numerous communities. It is growing still.

My conscious intention for my business was a huge success. But I also had an unconscious intent for my business, which I just recently realized. My store provided me with a place of quiet solitude to channel this book. Higher self and self made this a joint venture of discovery. Success? I think so.

I started this chapter like I was addressing a recovery group. Well, I am in recovery. I am recovering from the negative emotions and trauma of being human. I have been virtually symptom-free for many weeks. I'm sure I will have days when being human will drag me down. But my heart is ready to make the leap. I'm not there yet, but I can see the light. The White Sisterhood has made their energy known to me and would like to enter at this time.

## Mother Mary

We would like to thank Julie for sharing the events of her life with you. We have been with her from the beginning of her life, and we are overcome with joy that she has finally become aware of our presence. Julie has informed you that we are also called The Mother Mary Group. We purposely represented ourselves to her as the White Sisterhood because of the religious friction there on Earth. You humans do love your drama. You need to know that The Mother Mary energy is not a singular entity but a blend of feminine goddess energies. This has been a difficult concept for you humans to accept. You see yourselves as individuals and find it almost impossible to view yourselves or anything else as part of a vast universal consciousness.

There is a huge mass consciousness on Earth that singles out one person or soul as Mother Mary. There are numerous names given to this goddess/feminine energy: Kuan Yin, Saravisti, Venus, Tara, Isis, and Gaia, to name but a few. They are as varied as the religions they represent.

## Mother-Love

Since the advent of Christianity, Mother Mary has been one of the most beloved and popular religious figures because she represents a loving mother with human features and radiant clothing. She seems like a real person whom one can approach and talk to without fear. The Mary figures as portrayed in religious art are a doorway to the Creator. For example, the familiar figure of the Virgin of Guadalupe of Mexico is actually a veil that has been parted, a dimensional opening. Through such a doorway, people are going to move into Love—Mother-Love. Love's true essence is Mother-Love, with the most powerful image on Earth being that of a mother with an infant in her arms or at her breast. This Love will change the world.

The closest thing to such Mother-Love you seem to be able to come to on Earth is one person's Love for another person.

## Mary, a Multidimensional Being

Many people around the world speak for Mother Mary, not just one or two. Many different aspects of Mother Mary's teachings come through different people. The message in this book is from the multidimensional Mary, the feminine/goddess aspect that has yet to be heard. It is an aspect that people are now ready to hear, an aspect your hearts have been crying for. These words will resonate with many, but not with everyone.

Some of you are too stuck in the masculine energy. The masculine energy encases your heart like the shell of a walnut. But walnut shells can be broken. Your heart needs to be broken. Think what a broken heart means. It means opening yourself to true feelings and emotions. We need to break through the stoic, repressive shells enshrouding your heart.

## The Superconductors

The people who channel our energy act as superconductors. When we connect with them, it is like plugging into an electrical outlet. Each of these electrical beings acts as a transmitter, sending out a positive feminine energy field. Anyone and anything within fifty feet of these individuals is encompassed by our energy. This is how the transformation begins. Energy can enter into even the smallest of cracks. As you interact with your fellow man, tendrils of light energy reach out between you. When the light encounters a resistant shell around a heart, it searches for that opening. Once Love has its foot in the door, it is only a matter of time before the shell explodes and sets free the light trapped inside. This process continues in a domino effect, light seeking light.

## Earth's Great Mother Essence

Your own planet Earth is a living, feminine being with a great Mother Essence deep down in her core. She is bound and imprisoned by male control and harnessed like a slave so that her magnetic emotional energy can be used to keep people in control through the Old Structure set up by the dark cousins. Mother Earth expresses this male control force as a part of everyone's DNA. Not just men but also women suppress this female essence. They do not let it out for fear of how society will turn against them.

As the feminine Love energy spreads throughout mankind, so will it begin emanating more easily from Mother Earth. Re-member, man is a reflection of Mother Earth. As the shells around the heart of mankind crack, so too will the shell of the Earth. The cracks in Mother Earth will be a reflection of the emergence of the feminine Love energy in mankind. This is the key to the severity of the coming Earth changes. If mankind surrenders the male ego peacefully, Mother Earth will evolve gently. But if mankind resists and is violently opposed to the change, then Earth will reflect that violence in her evolution. As we told you before, no matter what, the Earth will continue her evolution.

## A Great Change Coming

A change is coming—a great change. You have been sleepwalking. Now you are coming awake. The increasing consciousness of the people will cause the shift for which you have been waiting. Love is going to make negative things move back. Things that do not want to be in this Love need to move back— to get off the planet. Loving people are holding unloving people on the planet, hoping to change them. Now they need to let them go. It is not up to you to change anyone. Re-member, Earth is a planet of free will. Simply show off your

Love. It is each individual's choice to change or not change. Maybe it is a part of their contract not to change.

## Mary's Blessings

Our blessings to all people who are open to our Love are going to be like cleansing water washing the planet. Some blessings will clear heart blocks. Different people will have different roles in the times to come. Some will send Love, some will receive Love, and some will both send and receive the Love frequency.

Some will allow this higher frequency of Love to flow from their hands or through their mouths. Some who receive the blessings will find themselves in tears and will at last be able to cry and express the sorrow they have held within themselves, and they will finally be able to heal. They will receive, and they will be given Love and light in their magnetic centers—their hearts. The Love frequency will penetrate and integrate into their beings.

## Have Intent to Feel Blessed

In the past, loving people have made mistakes: for example, believing that the power of Love/God required sacrifice. This is not true. Love had misunderstandings about itself from the beginning. Love is now sorting itself out. Guilt and Love have been confused. Ask yourself, does blame exist in your heart where something else should be? How can this be changed?

Mother Mary and the White Sisterhood are sending out blessings to all of you, but many of you do not receive them. You need to have intent to feel blessed. Say it aloud with emotion, "I have intent to feel blessed." Say it about others, "I want you to feel blessed today."

## The Heart Intent Technique

A group of cells deep within the heart is a doorway to divine Love…to divinity. These cells need to be accessed by every human being. These cells have been blocked by the powers-that-be on Earth. The technique to get in touch with this "Spark" is so simple that you may think it cannot be real. To get in touch with your own doorway of the heart, you must simply *have intent to feel Love… really to feel Love.*

Try to feel and resonate with others who may feel the same. Close your eyes and try it. Can you feel your heart inside you? Try to visualize it. Now try to visualize a spot in your heart where Love originates. Not your whole heart…just that spot deep inside. Do you feel anything? If you do, try to hold that feeling as long as you can.

If you do not feel anything, say aloud with emotion, "I intend to feel Love! I intend to feel Loved!" Your heart knows what to do. Keep this intent going for two minutes, whether or not you feel anything, and especially if you *do not* feel anything. Do this "Heart Intent Technique" every day. Someday, you will feel something, if this is your true intent. How long will it take? You will be surprised.

People's hearts are ready to take their proper place. But when you first begin to do the Heart Intent Technique, you may feel a bit silly because it sounds so simple and like a rather strange thing to do, at that. Then nothing happens. Have faith. It will happen. You will have a response. For some, it will come sooner than for others.

You need to know that what you are doing is something of brilliance, because true brilliance comes from simplicity. Let that be a principle for you to live by—*Simple is brilliant.*

## Sacrifice Not Necessary

Did you know that a great many people on Earth today feel that in order to be in the Creator's grace, in order to live as the Creator wants them to, they must sacrifice? This is not true. The Source of Love does not require sacrifice. Sacrifice damages the heart. The heart has better ways to live in the Creator's Love. Most of you who believe in sacrifice are caught up in the great illusion, the illusion that the Source of Love has to be in one place. But it is not so. The Source is multidimensional and can be in more than one place at a time.

How many of you are in sacrifice? How much of it do you like? Are you afraid to let go of it? Do you feel obligated to make sacrifices? Is this comfortable for you, or do you believe that feeling uncomfortable is part of the sacrifice pattern? That the worse you feel, the better Creator will like you? Or, if you sacrifice enough, you will be in a state of grace? *Creator does not want you to sacrifice!* There has been an enormous misunderstanding about sacrifice.

Many saints of the past sacrificed their health, their worldly goods, and even their lives for the love of Creator. Did they attain this love? Even Mother Teresa admits to a terrible emptiness throughout her life. From the start, she felt that she didn't deserve Creator's Love, so she sacrificed herself, not only to help Creator's lowliest creatures but also to gain a sense of worthiness. Although she helped thousands of diseased and forsaken people during her service to Creator, she was not fulfilling herself. It is a wonderful thing to give Love, but it is equally important to allow Love into your being.

## Focus on Love

People need to focus on Love—not sacrifice, not hate, not revenge. The force of Love needs to grow and grow throughout your planet. Humanity is not yet over the 50% point where Love becomes the controlling force. Once people reach over 50%, even 51%, they will change. They will either change or leave. When the majority of people allow Love into their beings, a great shift will occur on Earth.

On the other hand, loving people have to accept that others may not be able to change. They should not hold judgments against them. Many people have not had enough time to evolve to the state of consciousness that they need to enable them to make the shift. All is correct, no matter which point you may be at. Use prayer and intent. Do not use sacrifice. The structure of sacrifice will damage you. Say "no" to it. Those who know and recognize their mission here as they read these words must remove the implanted obligation of sacrifice. The Source of Love does not require it.

## Unseen Sacrifice Patterns

People still believe that "if you sacrifice enough, you will enter into a state of grace." This is a false sacrifice implanted by the false god that is in an ego-centered place in your being. All of you have unseen sacrifice patterns. This is not how it should be. There needs to be an end to sacrifice. Sacrifice is not going to heal you or the world.

Mother Teresa had an enduring pattern. She made herself endure no matter what. Enduring itself contains sacrifice. Enduring the pain of sacrifice is not going to allow healing. The world is full of sacrifice. Land is being sacrificed for people. Dolphins are being sacrificed for tuna. Money is being sacrificed to gain Creator's Love. Creator does not require sacrifice or surrender because of sacrifice. Give because you want to give. Give because it makes you feel good. Know this: you are worthy, no matter what!

## Sacrifice, an Old Pattern

The Old Structure of the dark cousins on your planet was based on sacrifice. Many of the high spiritual beings and masters who came to Earth in the past based their lives on sacrifice. Their greatest sacrifice was their own lives. Most were male, and they sacrificed their lives in the end, the ultimate denial. They did not realize they had parts of themselves in shadows or clouds. They suppressed their feelings. These high spiritual beings are still alive but in a different dimension. The world will change as they move through their shadows, not pushing them away but feeling, instead, the lost soul they created unconsciously by denying their feelings. Many of your religious people sacrifice their sexuality in hopes of achieving a state of grace.

## Words Carry Vibrations

Sacrifice has stolen something from good. Good has denied itself through its involvement with sacrifice. "Good" was once a powerful word but has become diluted because of its use in describing sacrifice. This will change when you listen to your heart and not your brain. Words do make a difference. Each word you utter carries a vibration that is heard and felt on Earth and beyond. When these vibrations heal and change, you will change, and the Earth will change.

Now is the time to release your own deep, dark feelings. When dark feelings come up, let them out with sounds. Speak aloud. Cry. Moan. Ask Spirit to come in and heal them. Have intent to open the dimensional doorway to your heart. Let joy and happiness flow in and out. Then you will know that sacrifice is not necessary, and that the only thing that counts is Love. Spirit's greatest wish for you is that you allow yourself to be open to Love and allow that Love to flow to others. Here is a mantra for you:

**Evolving Into Love Mantra**

> *I allow Love to flow into my being.*
> 
> *I allow Love to flow through me*
> 
> *to others.*
> 
> *Like a butterfly, I welcome*
> 
> *the metamorphosis.*
> 
> *I am evolving into Love with Love.*

## Allowing

We cannot stress enough the importance of *allowing*. If any word reached out and grabbed your attention in the reading of this book, we pray that it was the word *allow*. The game of life on Earth revolves around *allowing*. Re-member, Earth is the planet of free will, of choice. When you choose something, what is it you are doing? You are *allowing* that person, thing, or ideal into your life. *Allowing* is choice, so we hope you choose to *allow*. Let us look at some things you can attain through *allowing*.

> **A**…abundance
> 
> **L**…Love
> 
> **L**…living
> 
> **O**…ownership
> 
> **W**…worthiness

## Abundance

You surround yourselves with many roadblocks against abundance. If you were to allow true abundance into your lives, you would indeed have it all. Do not set limits on what abundance is. Abundance wears many faces. It is much more than wealth. If you were to view abundance with your whole vision, you would see that it brings you all your heart's desires. If you *allow* the many faces of abundance, you will have not only an abundance of wealth but also an abundance of hope, friends, love, joy, and more. Think of abundance as a train stretching into the sunset, each car carrying your life's joys.

## Love

*Allowing* Love into your lives has been a recurring theme throughout this book. *Allow* your physical self to give and receive Love, and *allow* your spiritual self to do the same. Re-member, Love is the key that unlocks all your doors. Love paves your road to enlightenment, and the Light of Love guides you home.

## Living

*Allow* yourself to live, really live. Feel life. Taste life. Smell life. You came into life to live. Do not sleepwalk through life. If you only get that one spontaneous moment to live life to its fullest, do it. Enjoy it. Re-member it.

## Ownership

We hear you thinking, what can they mean by ownership? Ownership means, "to take possession of." We want you to claim ownership of self. When you *allow* ownership of self, you create unity within. Many of you splinter yourselves into pieces. You do not recognize or lay claim to the aspects of yourself that you feel are lacking in some ways or perceive as negative. You even try to segregate these aspects from Creator. The aspects that you do not like are the reflections of the hurt child inside. When a child does something out of favor, do you shun that child and disown him? Of course not. You forgive and embrace. We say, *allow* ownership of self. Integrate and *allow* the divine light of All That Is to permeate your whole being.

## Worthiness

You are worthy! *Allow* yourself to feel worthiness. You carry a Spark of Creator inside you. You are divine individuals, and we lay our heads at your feet, honoring the difficult task you have undertaken. You are no less magnificent than Jesus, Mohammed, or Buddha. They came to Earth, as did other prophets—not to be worshipped, but to show you an example of who you really are. Once you *allow* yourselves to feel worthy, watch for the miracles to happen around you. Miracles are a manifestation of the magic you hold within.

The manipulation of the dark cousins has caused you to empower the sad and self-defacing aspects of your being. When negative things happen to you, we have heard so many of you say, "I deserved that. I must have done something wrong. I guess I deserved that." When something good or wonderful happens to you, you deny it. You say, "I don't deserve that. It must be a mistake. It must be for someone else." You find it much easier to accept something negative for yourselves than something positive. We say again, stop thinking like a human! *Allow* self-worth to work its magic inside you.

## Manifestation vs. Imagination

Do you feel the fullness of the cosmos? Is your inner light beginning to illuminate the road before you? Is your step lighter as you shed your three-dimensional shell? We shall answer "yes" for you. By *allowing* the information we have presented to you into your being, you have taken a huge step into the next dimension. You have entered the realm of limitless possibilities.

Throughout your trip on the road to enlightenment, you have been told many times to manifest your destiny. That time has passed. Manifesting no longer serves. Manifesting literally means "by the hand." Manifestation is a physically dense tool. Manifestation is stuck in the male energy. It is the left side of the brain's avenue to life. It even contains the word "man" in its makeup. Man empowers it.

Imagination is the new precept by which to live. Imagination and intuition are sister energies. They utilize the right brain and the heart. Imagination encourages and prompts you to make use of the magic within. Imagination is a spiritual tool, not a physical one. Re-member, you are evolving from a dense physical being into a spiritual light being. As a spiritual being, whatever you imagine, you can have. You can bring it into being. Re-member, you are creating Heaven on Earth, the most beautiful place you could ever imagine!

The White Sisterhood would like to thank you for *allowing* us to share our light with you. Re-member, the Light of Love illuminates the road before you, and all roads lead you Home. And so, it is…

*Speed Bumps on the Road to Enlightenment*

# About the Authors & Illustrator

Dr. Janice J. Beaty is a nationally recognized author in the field of early childhood education. For this book, she has turned her attention to the spiritual side of life, helping to bring in channeled information from a spiritual group known as the White Sisterhood. Her visits over the past 33 years to sacred sites in England; Ireland; Greece; Egypt; Mexico; Yucatan; Belize; Hawaii; Japan; Sedona, Arizona; and Ojo Caliente, New Mexico have opened her heart to receiving this information.

Julie Adams has experienced psychic connections her entire life, most recently leading psychic gatherings in northeastern Pennsylvania. She received direct information for this book from the White Sisterhood.

Spiritual artist Ernestine Madaleine has specialized for many years in drawing psychically created portraits of spirit guides and angels. For this book, and for the Spiritual Attunement Cards that accompany the book, she has used her unique talent to fashion illustrations that bring to life the words of the White Sisterhood.

# Did you like this book?

If you enjoyed this book, you will find more interesting books at

### www.CrystalDreamsPublishing.com

Please take the time to let us know how you liked this book. Even short reviews of 2-3 sentences can be helpful and may be used in our marketing materials. If you take the time to post a review for this book on Amazon.com, let us know when the review is posted and you will receive a free audiobook or ebook from our catalog. Simply email the link to the review once it is live on Amazon.com, your name, and your mailing address -- send the email to orders@mmpubs.com with the subject line "Book Review Posted on Amazon."

If you have questions about this book, our customer loyalty program, or our review rewards program, please contact us at info@mmpubs.com.

cdp
CRYSTAL DREAMS
publishing

*a division of Multi-Media Publications Inc.*

# Sailing on an Ocean of Tears

**By Donna Kendall**

Take a glimpse at the intimate and often heart-wrenching circum-stances of three women's lives as they become intertwined. Ruth is born to an impoverished, alcoholic and abusive family. She struggles to overcome her lot in life, only to discover that even well-intended decisions can lead us down the wrong path. She encounters Isabella, a vibrant Italian woman, whose deep compassion for others in need leads her away from her own chances for happiness. Bridget's hopes for happiness set her life on a course away from her native Ireland and the love of a childhood friend and into the arms of a brutal husband, intent on destroying her.

Each of their lives takes an integral path that leads them to a critical intersection where love, fate, and friendship help them to realize their greatest moment of truth.

ISBN-10:     1591460875
ISBN-13:     9781591460879
Price:       $14.95

Available from Amazon.com or your nearest book retailer.
Or, order direct at www.CrystalDreamsPublishing.com

# The Nurse and The Deputy

**By Rod Summitt**

When nurse Diane Rodgers moved to the Tri-County Area of Eastern Colorado, she was not looking for a new romance. She was only looking to escape the heartache of her broken relationship with Dr. William Stevenson. Although she had lived her whole life in Chicago, she quickly adapted to the small town life. Deputy Sheriff Shawn White met Diane in his official capacity on her first day in the area, but quickly decided he wanted to know her personally, not professionally. His early attempts to cultivate a relationship were carefully parried by Diane, but soon his persistence appeared to be paying off. However, a misunderstanding drove a wedge between them.

When Diane finds herself in a crisis and in need of help from Shawn in his official capacity, they find that they must also confront their personal relationship head on.

ISBN-10:     1591460840
ISBN-13:     9781591460846
Price:       $12.95

Available from Amazon.com or your nearest book retailer.
Or, order direct at www.CrystalDreamsPublishing.com.

# When Pasts Collide
## By Rod Summitt

When successful bookstore owner, Shelly Keel, is returning to her home in Boston from a business trip, she recognizes a fellow passenger on her flight as the man that broke her heart ten years before.

Although tempted, she resists confronting him and quickly goes about living her life which is very full except for love. A few weeks later, she comes face to face with him at a North Side restaurant. When he indicates that he would like to get together with her, she turns him down cold.

When problems at the bookstore create a need for a detective, Shelly's partner convinces her reluctantly to allow her old boyfriend to enter the scene in his professional capacity as a private detective. The close proximity and a developing relationship between Shelly's partner and David's associate draw them closer together. A sudden crises forces Shelly and David to confront their feelings for each other and their future.

ISBN-10:     1591460433
ISBN-13:     9781591460435
Price:       $12.00

Available from your nearest book retailer. Or, order direct at www.CrystalDreamsPublishing.com

## One: Memoir of a Manic Addict

**By Jennifer Marks**

A wild ride through the funhouse mirror revealing the blissful horror of drugs, the odd beauty of insanity, a huge sad impossible love, the brutal truth of growing up, of pain and loss and finding the strength to make sense of the senseless and the faith to go on with the burden of living.

This true story reflects upon the party life and the hip New York City drug scene, the distorted views and insane directions launched by an undiagnosed bipolar condition kept afloat with drugs, alcohol, food binges, sex, overspending, and an inability to touch land. The author grabs hold of her own life and comes to terms with who she really is when all the craziness is stripped away: she is every woman, a vulnerable human who got lost in darkness along the way and, by the grace of God, stumbled back into the light.

ISBN-10:     15914608675
ISBN-13:     9781591460862
Price:       $12.95

Available from Amazon.com or your nearest book retailer.
Or, order direct at www.CrystalDreamsPublishing.com.

Printed in the United States
132643LV00004B/4/P